New Daylight

Edited by **Sally Welch**

D0362831

September–December 2017

The Bible Reading Fellowship
15 The Chambers, Vineyard
Abingdon OX14 3FE
brf.org.uk

The Bible Reading Fellowship (BRF) is a Registered Charity (233280)

ISBN 978 0 85746 448 4
All rights reserved

This edition © The Bible Reading Fellowship 2017

Cover image and illustration on page 141 © Thinkstock

Distributed in Australia by MediaCom Education Inc, PO Box 610, Unley, SA 5061
Tel: 1 800 811 311 | admin@mediacom.org.au

Distributed in New Zealand by Scripture Union Wholesale, PO Box 760, Wellington
Tel: 04 385 0421 | suwholesale@clear.net.nz

Acknowledgements
The New Revised Standard Version of the Bible, Anglicised Edition, copyright © 1989,
1995 by the Division of Christian Education of the National Council of the Churches
of Christ in the USA. Used by permission. All rights reserved | The Holy Bible, New
International Version, Anglicised edition, copyright © 1979, 1984, 2011 by Biblica. Used
by permission of Hodder & Stoughton Publishers, an Hachette UK company. All rights
reserved. 'NIV' is a registered trademark of Biblica. UK trademark number 1448790. |
The Good News Bible published by The Bible Societies/HarperCollins Publishers Ltd,
UK © American Bible Society 1966, 1971, 1976, 1992, used with permission. | Scripture
quotations taken from the Amplified® Bible, Copyright © 1954, 1958, 1962, 1964, 1965,
1987 by The Lockman Foundation. Used by permission. (www.Lockman.org) | The
Revised Standard Version of the Bible, copyright © 1946, 1952, 1971 by the Division
of Christian Education of the National Council of the Churches of Christ in the United
States of America. Used by permission. All rights reserved. | Scripture quotations from
the Contemporary English Version. New Testament © American Bible Society 1991,
1992, 1995. Old Testament © American Bible Society 1995. Anglicisations © British &
Foreign Bible Society 1996. Used by permission. | Scripture taken from THE MESSAGE.
Copyright © 1993, 1994, 1995, 1996, 2000, 2001, 2002. Used by permission of NavPress
Publishing Group. | Scripture quotations taken from the Holy Bible, New Living
Translation, copyright © 1996, 2004, 2007, 2013. Used by permission of Tyndale House
Publishers, Inc., Carol Stream, Illinois 60188. All rights reserved. | Extracts from the
Authorised Version of the Bible (The King James Bible), the rights in which are vested
in the Crown, are reproduced by permission of the Crown's Patentee, Cambridge
University Press.

The Revised Common Lectionary is copyright © The Consultation on Common Texts,
1992 and is reproduced with permission. *The Christian Year: Calendar, Lectionary and
Collects*, which includes the *Common Worship* lectionary (the Church of England's
adaptations of the *Revised Common Lectionary*, published as the Principal Service
lectionary) is copyright © The Central Board of Finance of the Church of England,
1995, 1997, and material from it is reproduced with permission.

Printed by Gutenberg Press, Tarxien, Malta

Suggestions for using *New Daylight*

Find a regular time and place, if possible, where you can read and pray undisturbed. Before you begin, take time to be still and perhaps use the BRF Prayer on page 6. Then read the Bible passage slowly (try reading it aloud if you find it over-familiar), followed by the comment. You can also use *New Daylight* for group study and discussion, if you prefer.

The prayer or point for reflection can be a starting point for your own meditation and prayer. Many people like to keep a journal to record their thoughts about a Bible passage and items for prayer. In *New Daylight* we also note the Sundays and some special festivals from the Church calendar, to keep in step with the Christian year.

New Daylight and the Bible

New Daylight contributors use a range of Bible versions, and you will find a list of the versions used opposite. You are welcome to use your own preferred version alongside the passage printed in the notes. This can be particularly helpful if the Bible text has been abridged.

New Daylight affirms that the whole of the Bible is God's revelation to us, and we should read, reflect on and learn from every part of both Old and New Testaments. Usually the printed comment presents a straightforward 'thought for the day', but sometimes it may also raise questions rather than simply providing answers, as we wrestle with some of the more difficult passages of Scripture.

New Daylight is also available in a deluxe edition (larger format). Visit your local Christian bookshop or contact the BRF office, who can also give details about a cassette version for the visually impaired. For a Braille edition, contact St John's Guild, Sovereign House, 12–14 Warwick Street, Coventry CV5 6ET.

Comment on *New Daylight*

To send feedback, you may email or write to BRF at the addresses shown opposite. If you would like your comment to be included on our website, please email connect@brf.org.uk. You can also Tweet to @brfonline (please use the hashtag #brfconnect).

Writers in this issue

Harry Smart is an Anglican priest and has been a mental health and general hospital chaplain for many years. He has an interest in mindfulness and in labyrinths and has used them for patient and staff support.

Stephen Rand is an activist, writer and speaker who has worked with Tearfund and Open Doors. More recently he has been responsible for the public communications of the All Party Parliamentary Group on International Freedom of Religion or Belief.

David Winter is retired from parish ministry. An honorary Canon of Christ Church, Oxford, he is well known as a writer and broadcaster. His most recent book for BRF is *Heaven's Morning: Rethinking our destination*.

Steve Aisthorpe is a development worker for the Church of Scotland, encouraging mission and discipleship throughout the Highlands and Islands. He is the author of *The Invisible Church* (SAP, 2016).

Tony Horsfall is a freelance trainer and retreat leader based in Yorkshire, although now on a 'semi-retired' basis. He has written several books for BRF, the latest being *Spiritual Growth in a Time of Change*.

Veronica Zundel is an Oxford graduate, writer and columnist. She lives with her husband and son in north London. Her most recent book is *Everything I Know about God, I've Learned from Being a Parent* (BRF, 2013).

Nick Read is a Fellow of the Royal Agricultural Society. He was ordained in the Church of England in 1995. He is the Director of the Bulmer Foundation, a sustainable development charity based in Hereford.

Amanda Bloor is Priest in Charge of Bembridge, on the Isle of Wight, Assistant DDO for Portsmouth Diocese, and a Chaplain to Hampshire and Isle of Wight Army Cadet Force.

Margaret Silf is an ecumenical Christian committed to working across and beyond traditional divisions. She is the author of a number of books for 21st-century spiritual pilgrims, and a retreat facilitator.

Lakshmi Jeffreys is the rector of a parish just outside Northampton. She combines this with being a wife, mother, friend, dog-walker, school governor and various other roles, within and beyond the wider church.

Sally Welch writes...

The time of year covered by the September–December edition of *New Daylight* always presents challenges. We go from the bright (we hope) days of autumn sunshine, with memories of harvest plenty still fresh in our minds, into the darker days of winter and the cold, waiting time of Advent, finally relieved by the joyful news of Christmas at the very end of the issue. True to the season, this edition contains some very challenging notes, which help us look at the difficult times we might experience as individuals or as communities. Nick Read and Amanda Bloor use Advent as a time to explore the darker days of our lives, finding hope and exploring ways toward personal and community growth through the theme of wilderness and the book of Lamentations.

David Winter and Steve Aisthorpe go hand in hand in this issue as they look at two of the great themes of the Bible, which are still as pressing today as they were in New Testament times. David Winter examines the nature of justice in Matthew's Gospel and offers ways in which we might become more just in our dealings with ourselves and others. Sadly, Steve Aisthorpe's exploration of the concept of peace is still just as vital in our war-torn world, and he offers helpful and sensitive insights, founded on the peace that is so essential to Christ's nature and so vital for us all.

Lest we should be overwhelmed by the serious nature of our studies, Tony Horsfall gives us the reassurance of the many prayers that can be found in the Bible, and from Margaret Silf we get a delightful glimpse of the angels that populate both the Old and New Testaments, bringing hope and comfort. Margaret's notes culminate with that glorious host of angels singing out, 'Glory to God in the highest, and peace to his people on earth!'

I wish you all an interesting and joyful season of reading and prayer.

Sally Welch

The BRF Prayer

Almighty God,
you have taught us that your word is a lamp for our feet
and a light for our path. Help us, and all who prayerfully
read your word, to deepen our fellowship with you
and with each other through your love.
And in so doing may we come to know you more fully,
love you more truly, and follow more faithfully
in the steps of your son Jesus Christ, who lives and reigns
with you and the Holy Spirit, one God for evermore.
Amen

Mental health and the Bible

The Bible covers centuries of history. Over the last 200 years alone, with the development of mental health centres, psychoanalysis and pharmaceuticals, we may seem to have left the world of the Bible a long way behind. To look at characters within the Bible who may be understood to have suffered mental ill health is a sensitive task. It is important to take into account the changes in culture, spirituality and medical knowledge.

I worked for nearly 15 years as a mental health chaplain, and I am aware of the caution that is required before we make direct correlations between the attitudes within the ancient and classical world and the experience of people in our own. The Bible explores the relationships between God, nations and individuals, as well as the hope for healing in its broadest and deepest sense. We still have a need for that healing.

I am not a psychiatrist. My hope is that, through looking at figures within the Bible who may have had mental health problems, we may be able to discover that God works through our whole experience, and to see that healing is greater than simply a medical diagnosis.

People with mental health problems can be challenging. They witness, in their way, to the pain that our society often tries to hide. People with mental health issues may see the world differently. They can be more aware of the inadequacy of the way society measures itself or of what it considers to be most important. Friendship, love, kindness and care of the environment may be more cherished. The support of friends is greatly important.

Up to one in four people in the UK are estimated to have mental health problems, from depression to bipolar or schizophrenia. Many of us may know the edge of such experiences. It is so now and was so in biblical times. These experiences can be the place where we find God.

If you or someone you are close to has mental health problems, it is important to find support from people or groups you trust. In the UK, Mind, Sane and local groups can be good sources of information and help. A mental health chaplain may also be available to talk to at your local hospital.

HARRY SMART

Raising Cain

Cain rose up against his brother Abel and killed him... And the Lord said, 'What have you done? Listen... you will be a fugitive and a wanderer on the earth.' Cain said to the Lord, 'My punishment is greater than I can bear! Today you have driven me away from the soil, and I shall be hidden from your face; I shall be a fugitive and a wanderer on the earth.'

During my time as chaplain, I worked on two hospital forensic wards, with people who had committed crimes because of their illness. Offered an opportunity for longer working relationships and more in-depth work, I was able to join in conversations during activities such as art groups. One artist had moving insights into himself and expressed them in beautiful pictures of animals and in illustrated prayers. Communion services, too, presented an opportunity for discussion and reflection on the relevance of the Bible reading. There was something almost monastic about the single-sex wards, where people were trying to come to terms with their destructive behaviours or reflect on how they might live when they left.

Guilt itself can become destructive, and there seems to be little hope for Cain in this story. Mental illness can become a cage without a key. I remember one man who could not forgive himself for what he had done, despite the circumstances. We as staff tried to encourage him to forgive himself, but he found it so hard.

We may carry a sense of guilt that we cannot let go. It can even separate us from the source of hope, the support of others and the love of God. But there is hope. Cain's son Enoch went on to build a city, and another descendant invented ploughing. His was a sometimes dubious family house, but there is hope.

In my office I have an anastasis icon—a traditional painting from the Eastern church, with the descent of Jesus into hell as its subject matter. My icon shows Jesus raising Adam and Eve at the resurrection. He pulls them up out of the depths. Surely Christ's hand reaches out for Cain too.

HARRY SMART

'An evil spirit'

And the women sang to one another as they made merry, 'Saul has killed his thousands, and David his tens of thousands.' Saul was very angry, for this saying displeased him. He said, 'They have ascribed to David tens of thousands, and to me they have ascribed thousands; what more can he have but the kingdom?' So Saul eyed David from that day on. The next day an evil spirit from God rushed upon Saul, and he raved within his house, while David was playing the lyre, as he did day by day. Saul had his spear in his hand; and Saul threw the spear, for he thought, 'I will pin David to the wall.' But David eluded him twice. Saul was afraid of David, because the Lord was with him but had departed from Saul.

Saul is a complicated character who can be portrayed very sympathetically. He was reluctant to become king in the first place; then David, rather than one of his own sons, is named as his successor. No wonder he is angry! Jealousy of David's popularity burns within him. The contrast between the young Saul who won battles and rescued besieged cities and the later, troubled, jealous man who is afraid of the upstart David is extreme. He is crippled by self-doubt and a sudden overwhelming anger. Yet it is David who calms and soothes him with music (1 Samuel 16:23).

Many people in stressful jobs find that they come to a point when they can carry on no longer. Sometimes this ending can become positive: the trauma is overcome and a new career path may become available. But Saul is unable to accept that he is being passed over. He is in despair, and Samuel has abandoned him (1 Samuel 15:26). There is no precedent for abdication.

Many who undergo similar experiences remain affected by their breakdown. It is hard to reappraise oneself and change, daring to live differently. It leaves scars. For some, it isn't possible to make the change, and then families, finance and security are severely challenged. Homeless centres and doctors' surgeries tell many such stories.

What do I hang on to, that gets in the way of my spiritual well-being?
Can I, should I, take the risk to find a more fulfilling way of being?

HARRY SMART

The shame of it…

The king covered his face, and the king cried with a loud voice, 'O my son Absalom, O Absalom, my son, my son!' Then Joab came into the house to the king, and said, 'Today you have covered with shame the faces of all your officers who have saved your life today, and the lives of your sons and your daughters, and the lives of your wives and your concubines, for love of those who hate you and for hatred of those who love you. You have made it clear today that commanders and officers are nothing to you; for I perceive that if Absalom were alive and all of us were dead today, then you would be pleased.'

David's grief for his son is so great that his army general feels it threatens the kingdom. Joab accuses the king of losing all sense of perspective.

As a priest and chaplain, I have walked beside many who grieve and have witnessed the sense of chaos that can so disrupt and overwhelm them. Those in the throes of acute grief talk about the desire to be as they were before the death, or of wishing to remain at the graveside all the time, unable to accept a changed world. Grief is not mental illness but it can be overwhelming, and those who are overcome and paralysed by their feelings may need support.

David accepted Joab's comments and worked with them (2 Samuel 19:8). Bereavement, loss and, in a related way, mental illness can lead to a new and deeper knowledge of oneself and others. Life will never be the same again, but we can begin to live with a more genuine knowledge of ourselves and of our need for spiritual meaning in our lives. As I accompanied others through painful times of mourning and gradual acceptance, I often felt I was witnessing a type of resurrection. I saw slow but evident healing, and growth in self-knowledge and confidence, as well as a new expression of love for the deceased. There was death and loss, but new life too.

How can we and our churches support people who are grieving?
Can we allow people to be sad and still help them to hope?

HARRY SMART

Depression and communities

Be gracious to me, O Lord, for I am in distress; my eye wastes away from grief, my soul and body also. For my life is spent with sorrow, and my years with sighing; my strength fails because of my misery, and my bones waste away. I am the scorn of all my adversaries, a horror to my neighbours, an object of dread to my acquaintances; those who see me in the street flee from me.

King David's psalms are full of uncertainty, bordering on despair. He veers from trust to panic in what seems to be a wild and uncontrolled way.

We are more aware now of the frequency of mental illness within our population, and the churches have begun to respond more compassionately—for example, through the Church of England's Mental Health Matters initiative. However, there can still be a lack of understanding. I witnessed this in the attitude of a congregation towards a woman whose eyesight was failing. Once a regular churchgoer, she was increasingly unable to attend. Her fear intensified, as did her distress at becoming blind and the sense of isolation that the situation provoked. Most difficult of all was the belief of some people that her anger and depression over her condition were a sign that she lacked faith. They believed that she should trust God to help her overcome her blindness or be healed of it.

The psalms of David are very open about how hard it is to have trust. He does reach a point of calm, but his progress is fraught with questions. Human beings are by nature vulnerable and fragile—sometimes a difficult thing to remember. The first churches were gatherings of people from across society, most particularly those at its margins. Jesus' followers themselves were often uncertain or afraid, but Jesus welcomed them.

Fortunately, the blind woman's story ends well, as her congregation presented her with a talking Bible, thus affirming her status within the community and allowing her to continue to practise her faith. It was a visible sign of reaching out to be with her in the experience she was going through.

Think of someone you trust. How do they help you to share your vulnerability with them?

HARRY SMART

Nebuchadnezzar's dream

Upon my bed this is what I saw; there was a tree at the centre of the earth, and its height was great. The tree grew great and strong, its top reached to heaven, and it was visible to the ends of the whole earth. Its foliage was beautiful... There was a holy watcher, coming down from heaven. He cried aloud and said: 'Cut down the tree and chop off its branches, strip off its foliage and scatter its fruit... But leave its stump and roots in the ground.'

The book of Daniel is set during the exile from Judah, after Nebuchadnezzar has taken the nobility and the most skilled people into Babylon. Inevitably he is unpopular. However, he comes to respect the Jewish faith, particularly after the witness of the three men who survived the fiery furnace and the appearance of a fourth figure with them (Daniel 3). His dream, interpreted by Daniel, foretells a catastrophic decline, in which the loss of the beautiful tree presages the loss of sanity, leaving only a vestige of hope.

Our relationship with nature features strongly in our mental well-being. Hospitals can be alien places, far removed from natural surroundings. Yet the evidence is strong that connection with nature is vitally health-giving. The term 'nature-deficit disorder' has been given to the feeling of disconnection with the natural world that surrounds us.

Our churches have tended to avoid the theme of our relationship with nature, perhaps because it is wrongly perceived as pagan. I sometimes used to start services with a CD of birdsong, and meditation sessions used classical music with the sound of a babbling stream—recommended to me by a mental health services user.

The image of the remaining stump of a tree is a powerful one. An ill gentleman whom I know has planted fruit trees in his garden and rejoices in the birdlife he has attracted. Is that a waste of time in the face of mortality, or a prophetic act? For him, it is certainly the latter: his eyes brighten as he speaks of the new life that has come in. It is a legacy for the future.

The tree of life in Revelation 22:2 has the power of healing.
How do our churches celebrate the healing qualities of nature?

HARRY SMART

Nebuchadnezzar's madness

Immediately the sentence was fulfilled against Nebuchadnezzar. He was driven away from human society, ate grass like oxen, and his body was bathed with the dew of heaven, until his hair grew as long as eagles' feathers and his nails became like birds' claws. When that period was over, I, Nebuchadnezzar, lifted my eyes to heaven, and my reason returned to me. I blessed the Most High, and praised and honoured the one who lives for ever.

The 18th-century artist and poet William Blake's painting of Nebuchadnezzar graphically depicts the desperation and tortured nature of the king. Alienated from the human world, he becomes almost a beast, a chimera. This is the outworking of the dream of the chopped-down tree, which predicted the fall of the king who had persecuted his people.

Being exiled is a severe sentence; humiliating as it was for Nebuchadnezzar, however, the image of his being covered in the dews of heaven reminds us that God was never entirely absent. Eventually Nebuchadnezzar was able to return to his kingdom, his reason restored.

The history of mental health care can be seen to focus on the desirability of integration into society. Asylums were, theoretically, places where people could withdraw and find nurture and care. The Quakers developed places of light and open space where patients learnt or rediscovered what it was like to be treated with respect and to behave in a similarly respectful manner. This approach may seem a little patronising now, but it was a serious expression of an honouring of the Spirit of God in everyone.

There are times for each of us when it may be necessary to step aside from society, for our mental and spiritual well-being. Nebuchadnezzar's story inspired monks in Syria to turn to the desert as they searched for isolated places where they could renew their experience of God and abandon the things and ways of being that were extraneous. However, there are also times when we need to be reintegrated into our communities, either by our own efforts or with the help of others.

Nebuchadnezzar's health was restored after a time of isolation.
What would help you in a similar situation?

HARRY SMART

Where is God in all this?

Now there was a great wind, so strong that it was splitting the mountains and breaking rocks in pieces before the Lord, but the Lord was not in the wind; and after the wind an earthquake, but the Lord was not in the earthquake; and after the earthquake a fire, but the Lord was not in the fire; and after the fire a sound of sheer silence. When Elijah heard it, he... went out.

How do we keep a sense of direction in our lives? Elijah felt isolated and his work seemed to be in vain, so he retreated into the desert to take stock.

Several years ago, I met a highly intelligent scientist. He had previously stopped taking his medication and become quite seriously ill. Then he had been reunited with his wife, on the condition that he kept taking his medication, and had begun to make a good recovery. He was supported by a quiet inner voice that encouraged him, spoke of God's love for him and sustained him. He had a strong sense of faith, so it was bewildering when the voice stopped giving him compassionate support and began telling him to stop taking the medication. He spoke with me about it. To follow its instruction now would be to put his marriage and health in jeopardy. He understood the change in the voice as an aspect of his mental illness.

He listened deeply within himself to discern where God was leading him. He had a strong sense of the caring presence of God, especially in renewing the relationship with his family. God was still with him, in a presence more loving than the voice had become.

Research shows that many people hear voices. For some, the voices may be of abusers from their past or associated with highly traumatic episodes in their lives. Others, however, may hear positive voices, which can be encouraging and supportive. It is the negative voices that receive more publicity. People who speak about their voices may greatly lack self-confidence and may be very vulnerable to those who might not treat them with respect and care, including some from a faith perspective.

Discernment is so important. The scientist held to his understanding of a loving and healing God and received support from mental health professionals. How do we practise discernment in our spiritual lives?

HARRY SMART

Beside himself

Then [Jesus] went home; and the crowd came together again, so that they could not even eat. When his family heard it, they went out to restrain him, for people were saying, 'He has gone out of his mind.' And the scribes who came down from Jerusalem said, 'He has Beelzebul, and by the ruler of the demons he casts out demons.'

Christopher Smart, a poet who was confined in the 1700s for insanity, wrote a poem called 'Jubilate Agno'. It contains beautiful verses about his cat Jeffrey and disturbing lines about his ill-treatment by warders. Smart appeals for mercy because even Jesus was described as 'beside himself'.

I remember a woman who became particularly ill and was put into the seclusion room. Though isolated from other patients, she was safer because there were no breakable items in the room which could have caused harm. Seclusion can be a frightening experience; patients should be regularly checked, and often they do receive a lot of support. Some may feel abandoned, however, or may be distressed by the serious nature of their illness. It can be traumatising. This woman spoke of feeling that she was walking with Jesus on the path to crucifixion.

Jesus' family feared for him. He was behaving strangely, challenging people, upsetting convention and getting angry; his followers were a mixed bunch. The family thought he was mad. He talked about the kingdom of God but didn't fit in with religious convention and practice. Unlike John the Baptist, he didn't fast; he healed people on the sabbath and was gathering more and more followers.

Our idea of sanity and health can become very exclusive. What can we learn from those who may be ill? In Mark 1:40–42, we read of a leper being healed by Jesus. Though an outcast, he recognised Jesus as someone who would welcome and heal. Later we hear the parable of the sower: the seed that is scattered and allowed to grow, nurtured and encouraged, yields a good harvest (Mark 4:3–20). These are insightful comments on how we can measure the prophetic nature of what might be derided as illness.

Can we be aware of Jesus with us in our suffering? Can that awareness be a source of hope?

HARRY SMART

Binding up the hurt

As [Jesus] stepped out on land, a man of the city who had demons met him. For a long time he had worn no clothes, and he did not live in a house but in the tombs. When he saw Jesus, he fell down before him and shouted at the top of his voice, 'What have you to do with me, Jesus, Son of the Most High God?'

The Gerasene demoniac isn't given a name. He is remembered because of his illness and because of Jesus' response. Like King Saul, he is overcome by anger and despair. He has been cast out of his society and dwells among the dead. Perhaps something has died within him—the hope for kindness or welcome or new life. Mental illness can separate people from friends and communities: relationships don't always survive. Many of us could develop mental health problems, and factors such as unemployment, poverty, prejudice and isolation greatly increase the possibility.

There is a deep sadness and desperation about the demoniac in this story. Some of that sadness is expressed in the physical harm he does to himself. For some people, self-harm can bring a release of tension. It can be done through drugs, sex, alcohol or dangerous driving, as well as through cutting, but there is always a sad destructiveness there. People may feel suicidal without wanting to kill themselves, or they may be plagued by memories. Times when they are bound up and cared for may be the only occasions when they feel noticed.

Jesus, who has just calmed a storm on the lake (Luke 8:22–25), deliberately meets with the man. 'What have you to do with me?' asks the demoniac, as if he deserves no attention at all. Why would Jesus be concerned? But Jesus reaches into the dark, dead places, where the hurt is.

Jesus instructs the man to go home and to give thanks to God. He has experienced God through Jesus. Understandably, he wants to follow his healer, but perhaps Jesus feels that there has been enough isolation in the sick man's life. So he is told to return to his home and city and speak of what has happened.

Can you sometimes be self-destructive? When in your life have you felt free of those self-destructive patterns?

HARRY SMART

Jonah

I remember it well. It was one of my favourite Sunday school songs, all about the tale of Jonah and the whale (I loved the way 'ocean' rhymed with 'notion'). If you recall it, especially the energetic actions, feel free to let that memory live again—perhaps in the privacy of your own home!

Some of you will instantly want to point out it wasn't a whale that swallowed Jonah; it was a 'big fish'. But for most, I suspect, the song sums it up: it's a great children's Bible story, and probably not one that we think about much after Sunday school.

Jonah is one of the twelve 'minor prophets', those hard-to-find books at the end of the Old Testament. But as a book, as a minor prophet, Jonah is different. The others speak the word of the Lord primarily to the people of God (and sometimes other nations as well) for a particular time in their history. Most of the text is taken up with what God wants to say through the prophet. In Jonah, however, God speaks to him in the first verse, and that triggers a story. It's a story of tragedy, comedy, pathos and truly remarkable events.

Academics have debated extensively over whether Jonah is a true story. Did it really happen? If so, when did it happen? Was there a big fish? Was it big enough to swallow a man? Can a man live for three days inside a fish? There is a prophet called Jonah mentioned elsewhere in the Bible (2 Kings 14:25), where the fulfilment of one prophecy is highlighted, but that's as far as the evidence goes.

Even though I used to be a history teacher, I'm not sure the history is what matters most in the book of Jonah. It is certainly about truth. It's a story written not just to entertain but to tell us something important, something true. In the next 14 days we'll discover that it's not so much about a big fish, or even about Jonah: it's about God. They story teaches us how God treats ordinary people, awkward people, people who do, and don't do, what they are told. That's what makes it a true story, one worth reading, and one for grown-ups, not just Sunday school children.

So come and listen to my tale…

STEPHEN RAND

'Arise, go'

Now the word of the Lord came to Jonah the son of Amittai, saying, 'Arise, go to Nineveh, that great city, and cry against it; for their wickedness has come up before me.'

There's no great introduction, just the word 'Now'… and the story starts. The two main characters are there in the first verse: God speaks to Jonah. To the Jewish audience that first heard this story, this opening would have come as no surprise: God speaks through prophets. But the announcement of what God said would have caused a gasp of amazement, even consternation. Nineveh? Go to Nineveh?

Nineveh was the enemy. No one could argue that it was not a great city. From 701BC until its dramatic fall in 612BC, when it was reduced to ruins by the Medes and Babylonians, Nineveh was the capital city of the Assyrian empire. This same Assyrian empire had a policy of deporting captives and replacing them with foreigners—a policy that devastated the ten northern tribes of Israel when they were defeated by Assyria in 721BC.

The prophet Nahum called Nineveh 'a city of bloodshed', full of 'endless cruelty' (Nahum 3:1, 19, NRSV). The first hearers of the story knew all about the wickedness of Nineveh, but why would God want Jonah to go there, even if his mission was to 'cry against it'?

One reason is that God is the God of the whole world, not just the people of Israel. Nineveh's wickedness was not overlooked; it had not been forgotten. Jonah was told to get up and go to the enemy, the place full of wickedness, the place full of people who cared nothing about God or about goodness—but that is what God is like. The apostle Paul puts it like this: 'God demonstrates his own love for us in this: while we were still sinners, Christ died for us' (Romans 5:8).

There is a challenge here for us, the church. We are still being asked to get up and go to wicked people in terrible places. There can be no 'untouchables', no 'no-go' areas for God's love and God's people.

Loving God, help me to be alert to your call to go to the unloved, and to be ready to answer it.

STEPHEN RAND

Taking flight, going down

But Jonah rose to flee to Tarshish from the presence of the Lord. He went down to Joppa and found a ship going to Tarshish; so he paid the fare, and went on board, to go with them to Tarshish, away from the presence of the Lord.

God told Jonah, 'Arise, go to Nineveh.' Jonah rose... and set off in the opposite direction. Nineveh was in the east; Jonah was desperate to go west—so desperate that he was prepared to pay. The writer mentions Tarshish three times, to underline Jonah's preferred destination. Scholars are not agreed about where it was; most think it was probably on the south-west coast of Spain. Isaiah 66:19 includes it in a list of places that are distant, far away, that have not heard of God's fame or seen his glory.

That was Jonah's hope: God would not be there. The writer is very clear. Jonah was not anxious to visit the beaches of the Costa del Sol; he wanted to escape the presence of the Lord. He should have known that it wasn't possible. King David had asked, 'Where can I flee from your presence?... If I take the wings of the morning and settle at the farthest limits of the sea, even there your hand shall lead me, and your right hand shall hold me fast' (Psalm 139:7, 9–10, NRSV). In modern parlance, 'You can run, but you can't hide.' However, note that it is God's guidance and protection that cannot be escaped.

The story at this stage gives no clue why Jonah chose to run. We have no idea whether he was frightened or rebellious or just didn't like Assyrians. But the choice of language to describe his disobedience is informative: he 'went down'. First he went down to Joppa, and before long he would be going down even further. Disobedience to God often leads to a downward spiral; obedience is the only way up.

I've never taken a boat to try to avoid doing what God wants, but I suspect that we all have our subtler techniques for disobedience—pretending we don't understand, putting it off, or allowing ourselves to get distracted. However we duck and dive, we risk disaster.

The hymn we sang at my baptism put it simply:
'Trust and obey, for there's no other way...'

STEPHEN RAND

Who is responsible?

Then the Lord sent a great wind on the sea… All the sailors were afraid and each cried out to his own god. And they threw the cargo into the sea to lighten the ship. But Jonah had gone below deck, where he lay down and fell into a deep sleep. The captain went to him and said, 'How can you sleep? Get up and call on your god! Maybe he will take notice of us so that we will not perish.' Then the sailors said to each other, 'Come, let us cast lots to find out who is responsible for this calamity.' They cast lots and the lot fell on Jonah.

Did Jonah really think he could escape that easily? In no time, God was engaging with him again, and this time he used his creation to do the talking. It must have been a terrible storm. Hardened, experienced sailors were terrified. They did what so many people do in desperate circumstances: they cried out to their gods. Only one person seemed unconcerned: Jonah was fast asleep.

His disobedience had brought the whole crew into mortal danger. This is an important truth. Our society believes there is no victimless crime, and, even if our behaviour is not illegal, disobedience to God's way will almost certainly bring damage, even disaster, to others. We see it in families, in churches and in society at large. Living in God's world God's way is not only the right way to live, it is the best way to live.

Jonah's shipmates were convinced that the storm ('this evil', v. 7, RSV) was someone's fault: 'Who is responsible?' But while the storyteller is crystal clear that God had produced the storm, this does not mean that every storm, of whatever kind, is someone's fault, provoking a divine act of punishment. In fact, redemption, not punishment, was God's purpose; the storm was prompted by love and mercy, not judgement.

Jonah was awoken. Did he notice that the captain used the same command that God had used: 'Arise'? The sailors resorted to an ancient way of making decisions: roll the dice and trust God for the right answer. They got it.

Lord, help me to discern when you are speaking to me
through the storms of life.

STEPHEN RAND

Cause and effect

Then they said to him, 'Tell us on whose account this evil has come upon us...' And he said to them, 'I am a Hebrew; and I fear the Lord, the God of heaven, who made the sea and the dry land.' This terrified them and they asked, 'What have you done?' (They knew he was running away from the Lord, because he had already told them so.) The sea was getting rougher and rougher. So they asked him, 'What should we do to you to make the sea calm down for us?' 'Pick me up and throw me into the sea,' he replied, 'and it will become calm. I know that it is my fault.'

They are in the middle of a terrible storm. Their prayers have failed. They have rolled the dice, and the finger of fate has pointed at Jonah. Here the story takes an almost comic turn. The sailors surely can't have been very surprised it was Jonah: he had already told them he was running away from God. But now they need to know more, and begin a rapid-fire interrogation: 'What kind of work do you do? Where do you come from? What is your country? From what people are you?' (v. 8b, NIV).

Jonah's answer terrifies them. They discover he is a Hebrew, and they also discover the God they are all dealing with—the one with real power. Jonah says that this is the God he 'fears'. To 'fear' God can mean to worship him (as in the NIV translation). Psalm 33:8 (AMP) says, 'Let all the earth fear the Lord [revere and worship Him]; let all the inhabitants of the world stand in awe of Him.' It also means to obey God: 'Fear the Lord your God as long as you live by keeping all his decrees and commands' (Deuteronomy 6:2, NIV).

There was a yawning gap between Jonah's words and the reality. But then we all turn up at church to worship one Sunday—and the following Sunday we are confessing our sins once again. Some, sadly, don't seem to realise the contradiction between words and behaviour. The only way we can truly worship God is to obey him.

Jonah concludes that his sin demands sacrifice: 'Throw me overboard...'

Lord, help me to worship you in obedient service every hour of every day.

STEPHEN RAND

21

The crew converted

Instead, the men did their best to row back to land. But they could not, for the sea grew even wilder than before. Then they cried out to the Lord, 'Please, Lord, do not let us die for taking this man's life. Do not hold us accountable for killing an innocent man, for you, Lord, have done as you pleased.' Then they took Jonah and threw him overboard, and the raging sea grew calm. At this the men greatly feared the Lord, and they offered a sacrifice to the Lord and made vows to him.

They have pinpointed the man to blame; he has instructed them to throw him overboard and their problem will be ended. But it turns out that they fear God more than Jonah does. They would rather break their backs rowing against the storm than take his life—but the sea grows wilder. God's plan and purpose for Jonah is not to be diverted.

Their prayer suggests that their concern is more for themselves than for Jonah. They know that they are collateral damage, bystanders caught up in a tempestuous conversation between God and his prophet. Pilate washed his hands before condemning Jesus; these sailors pray a kind of life insurance prayer.

They recognise and articulate a key concept that lies at the heart of this story: 'You, Lord, have done as you pleased' (v. 14). If God is God, that's the point: he can do as he pleases. But because God is God, what he pleases will always be just and right. It takes Jonah much longer than the sailors to understand this.

So Jonah gets his wish, and over the side he goes. The storm ends and the sailors recognise God at work. At the very least, they can see that their gods have been unable to still the raging sea. Perhaps their sacrifice and their vows are little more than superstitious responses to a deeply unsettling event—or perhaps their encounter with God's power has refocused their thinking completely. I can't help wondering if they ever heard that God rescued Jonah.

Do people ever see God at work in me and through me, enough to convince them that he should be worshipped and obeyed?

STEPHEN RAND

God's unusual rescue

Now the Lord provided a huge fish to swallow Jonah, and Jonah was in the belly of the fish three days and three nights.

God has 'hurled' a wind into the sea to create a storm; the sailors have 'hurled' their cargo overboard, shortly followed by their high-risk passenger. Now comes a period of peace, a chance for reflection—inside a huge fish! Once again, the writer indicates clearly that this was not a lucky coincidence. God was still proactive, on Jonah's case: he was the one who 'provided' the fish. The Hebrew word means 'appointed' or 'prepared'.

Jonah may well have thought something along the lines of 'Out of the frying-pan, into the fire'. He is unlikely to have recognised the fish as a saviour; one moment he'd have thought he was drowning, the next that he was being eaten. He may not even have had time to think, initially, that he was experiencing the very judgement he had been asked to declare to the city of Nineveh.

Those who believe in miracles will recognise Jonah's rescue as a miracle. In 2016, a Spanish fisherman claimed to have survived inside a blue whale for three days—but it was not widely reported. Hard-bitten journalists were not convinced. However, one commentator prefers the possibility that 'The Fish' was a pub where Jonah recovered after swimming ashore. Another, seeking meaning perhaps a little closer to the story, suggests that three days and three nights was, in some Near Eastern mythologies, the length of the journey to the underworld.

The fish is not the point of the story. It is mentioned twice, but there is no graphic description of its insides. The story is not being written to maximise dramatic effect but to underline theological truth. The huge fish simply indicates the grace of God giving Jonah a second chance, the start of a new life when he thought he was dead.

There are many people who will tell of a dramatic experience that prompted them to think about the purpose of life and their relationship with God. Lives are still being changed by brushes with death.

What does it take for me to find the time to think about my relationship with God?

STEPHEN RAND

In my distress

From inside the fish Jonah prayed to the Lord his God. He said: 'In my distress I called to the Lord, and he answered me. From deep in the realm of the dead I called for help, and you listened to my cry. You hurled me into the depths... all your waves and breakers swept over me. I said, "I have been banished from your sight; yet I will look again towards your holy temple."'

Chapter 1 was full of dramatic action; chapter 2 is a prayer. It is a beautifully crafted prayer, full of literary excellence, which echoes some of the psalms of David. The cynic will doubt that such a poetic gem could originate inside a fish, but those same psalms were often written out of times of great danger and despair. The experience and the emotions were instant; possibly the crafting came later.

The Hebrew understanding of the universe was that it consisted of three storeys: heaven above; earth in the middle, floating on subterranean waters; and Sheol, the place of the dead, underneath. So Jonah's prayer comes from the experience of sinking into the depths, heading towards death.

This prayer is a statement of faith: the writer believes that God answers prayer. Whereas Jonah was desperate to escape from God, now he acknowledges that God hears his prayer from the most unlikely place: 'deep in the realm of the dead' (v. 1). Any active Christian life is built on the same conviction that God hears and answers prayer.

The prayer is also a guide to faith. What should we do when we are in distress? 'Call on the Lord.' Where should we turn when all else seems to have failed? 'I will look again towards your holy temple', the place where we can meet with God. My conviction is that someone reading this will be feeling that, right now, all the waves and breakers are sweeping over them; perhaps even that they have been banished from God's sight. It is equally my conviction that God is listening to their cry.

Lord, thank you for hearing my cry. Thank you that there is no place too deep for you to reach down and grant me your presence and your assurance.

STEPHEN RAND

Salvation comes from the Lord

'But you, Lord my God, brought my life up from the pit. When my life was ebbing away, I remembered you, Lord, and my prayer rose to you, to your holy temple. Those who cling to worthless idols turn away from God's love for them. But I, with shouts of grateful praise, will sacrifice to you. What I have vowed I will make good. I will say, "Salvation comes from the Lord."' And the Lord commanded the fish, and it vomited Jonah on to dry land.

Jonah is now relieved, and glad, that there is nowhere he can escape from God's presence. His rebellion is over; he will now trust God for his life. He is now sure that the fish was not a deadly alternative to death by drowning, but a means of grace, a source of salvation.

So inside the fish he promises that he will be a changed person. He will make his sacrifices; he will keep his vows. He will no longer turn away from God's love, like 'those who cling to worthless idols' (v. 8). So what was Jonah's 'worthless idol'? Perhaps it was as simple as putting himself first, rejecting God's command and therefore his love. He has learned his lesson.

Can you hear the echo in the New Testament, where Jesus tells the story of the prodigal son? The young man was eating pigswill when he came to his senses and remembered that he had a father who loved him, despite his rebellion and disobedience. And when he turned and sought out his father, he received a wonderful welcome. That's what God is like. The fish is a sign of God's love and mercy.

Verse 10 is a favourite verse for many children. They love the grossness of the fish vomiting Jonah on to dry land. Three days of undigested Jonah? The fish was glad to be rid of him. But even this was in direct response to God's command. In the midst of death, Jonah had trusted God for his life. It wasn't the fish that saved Jonah: 'Salvation comes from the Lord' (v. 9).

Almighty Father, thank you for your love and mercy; thank you for your welcome when we turn to you. Thank you that repentance leads to forgiveness and new life. Amen

STEPHEN RAND

A second time

Then the word of the Lord came to Jonah a second time: 'Go to the great city of Nineveh and proclaim to it the message I give you.' Jonah obeyed the word of the Lord and went to Nineveh.

Inside the fish, Jonah had prayed, 'What I have vowed I will make good' (2:9). Another translation says, 'I will never worship anyone but you! For how can I thank you enough for all you have done? I will surely fulfil my promises' (LB). He does not have long to wait to be put to the test. The second command is exactly the same as the first: 'Arise, go to Nineveh, that great city…' This time there is no hesitation, let alone rebellion: Jonah obeys.

It is worth emphasising that having been saved in chapter 2, Jonah is straightaway given his marching orders in chapter 3. In the terms of this story, that is not surprising, but over the years I have been amazed at the number of people who call themselves Christians, who claim to have gratefully received God's offer of salvation through faith in Christ, and yet show no signs that their life has changed at all, let alone been committed to obedience to God.

The apostle Paul was faced with those who thought that, once saved, they could live how they liked, not how God liked. He responded, 'What, then? Shall we sin, because we are not under law but under God's grace? By no means!' (Romans 6:15, GNB). James was equally forceful in his letter: 'Faith by itself isn't enough. Unless it produces good deeds, it is dead and useless' (James 2:17, NLT). Or as Eugene Peterson puts the same verse in THE MESSAGE, 'Isn't it obvious that God-talk without God-acts is outrageous nonsense?'

With about one-third of the world's population claiming to be Christian, the world needs them to be Jonah version 2, not Jonah version 1—taking the name of Christ and doing what Christ would do. We are called to serve God in obedience, in our private life and our public life, in our home life and our work life—in every aspect of our life.

Promises made in adversity need to be kept in prosperity.

STEPHEN RAND

Would you believe it?

Nineveh was a very large city... Jonah began by... proclaiming, 'Forty more days and Nineveh will be overthrown.' The Ninevites believed God. A fast was proclaimed, and all of them, from the greatest to the least, put on sackcloth... The king of Nineveh rose from his throne, took off his royal robes, covered himself with sackcloth and sat down in the dust. This is the proclamation he issued in Nineveh: '... Let everyone call urgently on God. Let them give up their evil ways and their violence. Who knows? God may yet relent and with compassion turn from his fierce anger so that we will not perish.'

Jonah had taken on a task of epic proportions. The storyteller is at pains to underline just how big Nineveh was—an enormous city at the heart of a powerful and evil empire. Jonah was just one person, though one with a message from God.

The message was stark, a proclamation of judgement. But there was also a window of hope. There would be 40 days before their fate was sealed. Did the Ninevites deserve a stay of execution? No. But just as Jonah had been given three days of grace in the belly of the fish, God's grace was now extended to these evil foreigners.

This is what God is like. 'The Lord isn't slow about keeping his promises, as some people think he is. In fact, God is patient, because he wants everyone to turn from sin and no one to be lost' (2 Peter 3:9, CEV).

Then come four words that no listener or reader would have expected: 'The Ninevites believed God.' God's patience reaped a reward. God's word (not Jonah's preaching) provoked a positive response from the lowest to the highest—the whole city. Another miracle!

Their belief prompted immediate action—a massive all-encompassing fast of repentance. The king took the lead, his proclamation indicating that this was not a hollow religious ritual but a sign of intent. The fasting was to be matched by an end to their evil ways and violent behaviour: the outward sign had to represent spiritual reality.

Thank you for your patience with me, your grace shown to me, and the hope that both bring to me.

STEPHEN RAND

Repenting and relenting

When God saw what they did and how they turned from their evil ways, he relented and did not bring on them the destruction he had threatened.

The king of Nineveh had hoped, 'God may yet relent and with compassion turn from his fierce anger' (3:9). He understood that repentance—turning one's back on evil and beginning to live a good and godly life—is not an automatic passport to God's mercy, because God cannot be manipulated by human behaviour. 'I will have mercy on whom I will have mercy, and I will have compassion on whom I will have compassion' (Exodus 33:19).

He also understood the nature of God, who had announced himself to Moses as 'the Lord, the compassionate and gracious God, slow to anger, abounding in love and faithfulness, maintaining love to thousands, and forgiving wickedness, rebellion and sin. Yet he does not leave the guilty unpunished' (Exodus 34:6–7). The God revealed in the Bible is one who longs to bless his creation.

Some older translations of Jonah 3:10 suggest that God was the one who repented: 'God repented of the evil which he had said he would do to them' (RSV). Its updated version reads, 'God changed his mind about the calamity that he had said he would bring upon them' (NRSV). This is a good example of why it is helpful to use a modern translation! Our ancestors used 'repent' to indicate a change of mind; we tend to assume that it carries an admission of guilt. The Hebrew word here encompasses the concept of compassion. God was not feeling guilty about his judgement on Nineveh: it was entirely just, because of their wickedness. But he was feeling compassionate, because they were people made in his image who had thrown themselves on his mercy.

Aren't you glad that God is a God of mercy, one who relents? One who 'does not treat us as our sins deserve' (Psalm 103:10)? The one who sent his Son to die so that we could live?

'But the tax collector stood at a distance. He would not even look up to heaven. He brought his hand to his heart and prayed, "God, have mercy on me, a sinner"' (Luke 18:13, author's translation).

STEPHEN RAND

Jonah's anger

But to Jonah this seemed very wrong, and he became angry. He prayed to the Lord, 'Isn't this what I said, Lord, when I was still at home? That is what I tried to forestall by fleeing to Tarshish. I knew that you are a gracious and compassionate God, slow to anger and abounding in love, a God who relents from sending calamity. Now, Lord, take away my life, for it is better for me to die than to live.'

Jonah is not glad to see God's mercy; he's angry! Not just angry: he's incensed. Now he explains why he set off to Tarshish. He wasn't frightened for his own safety; he was frightened that God would be gracious to the hated Assyrians. That would be just too much.

The first readers of Jonah, those who first heard the story, would have completely understood. There would have been raised eyebrows when they heard that the Ninevites had believed, scorn and disbelief at their repentance and complete dismay when God relented from his judgement. They would have been with Jonah: these wicked, rapacious, slaughtering, kidnapping foreigners should get what they deserve. How dare God show *them* compassion?

How would we feel if we updated the story? Some will remember the story of Corrie ten Boom, who survived the concentration camp at Ravensbrück. After the war, she came face-to-face with a guard who said, 'Since that time, I have become a Christian. I know that God has forgiven me for the cruel things I did there, but I would like to hear it from your lips as well. Fräulein, will you forgive me?' (*The Hiding Place*).

Brother Andrew, the founder of Open Doors, suggested that Christians should pray for the members of ISIS, that they would repent and find forgiveness. For some, this was a bridge too far. You may be reading this, and feel that it is even more personal. Someone has hurt you, and you can't bring yourself to forgive them. The last thing you want is for God to forgive them. It would be so unfair; they shouldn't be allowed to get away with it.

---

*The Lord's Prayer is so pointed: 'Forgive us our sins,
as we forgive those who sin against us.'*

STEPHEN RAND

Still angry

But the Lord replied, 'Is it right for you to be angry?'… Then the Lord God provided a leafy plant and made it grow up over Jonah to give shade for his head to ease his discomfort, and Jonah was very happy about the plant. But at dawn the next day God provided a worm, which chewed the plant so that it withered… The sun blazed on Jonah's head so that he grew faint. He wanted to die, and said, 'It would be better for me to die than to live.' But God said to Jonah, 'Is it right for you to be angry about the plant?' 'It is,' he said. 'And I'm so angry I wish I were dead.'

Jonah's anger is still burning. He's convinced he is right and God is wrong: the Ninevites deserve to be destroyed. In fact, he thinks he might have persuaded God to do the decent thing, so he settles down on the hillside to get a really good view of the destruction. 'Will not the Judge of all the earth do right?' (Genesis 18:25).

The sun leaves Jonah burning on the outside as well as the inside. But God, who is indeed slow to anger, decides he will offer Jonah another chance to understand, since he seems to have forgotten the huge fish rescue. So God provides a shady plant—what one commentator calls 'a little gift of grace'. 'You have been… a shelter from the storm and a shade from the heat' (Isaiah 25:4).

After the mercy of the plant comes the worm of judgement. God is so unfair: he has refused to destroy the Ninevites, and now he is persecuting Jonah. If there is to be no justice in the world, Jonah might as well be dead. The last thing he wants is for his view of life to be undermined.

Paul writes, 'Let God change the way you think' (Romans 12:2, CEV). That's easier said than done. We all have ideas and attitudes that are at odds with God's character and revelation. We all need our minds transformed so that we can know 'what God's will is—his good, pleasing and perfect will' (NIV).

Dear God, when I know I'm right and you have got it all wrong…
please be gentle with me.

STEPHEN RAND

Tears in your eyes

But the Lord said, 'You have been concerned about this plant, though you did not tend it or make it grow... And should I not have concern for the great city of Nineveh, in which there are more than a hundred and twenty thousand people who cannot tell their right hand from their left—and also many animals?'

The story ends with a question. Who—or what—do I care about most? Jonah, dramatically rescued from a watery grave, who has seen a whole city respond to his preaching, is now focused on a leafy plant—or rather the loss of it.

When we get out of step with God, we can lose all perspective, concerned with minutiae, having no view of or interest in the big picture. It also works the other way: when we lose our perspective and focus on petty detail, we will all too easily find ourselves out of step with God.

God points out that the plant does not belong to Jonah, whereas, by implication, God is the creator not only of the plant but of the people and animals of Nineveh. That's why he is 'concerned' for them. 'The Lord is good to all; he has compassion on all he has made' (Psalm 145:9).

'Concerned' is a weak translation. The word means 'pity', 'have compassion', 'grieve over'. At its root it means 'to act with tears in one's eyes'. In the years I worked with Tearfund and Open Doors, I often prayed that I would not get so used to seeing suffering that my heart would get hardened and the tears cease to flow.

The story of Jonah reveals a God who acts with tears in his eyes. A God who loves the world so much that he sent his Son to die, so much that he offers forgiveness to Jonah, to Nineveh, to me, to you, to the whole world. If and when we receive that forgiveness, then a new story can start: God still says 'Arise, go.' Do we care enough? Are there tears in our eyes?

Lord, grant me your vision of your world and your Spirit of compassion. Keep my heart soft, my eyes moist, my feet walking, my hands open. Amen

STEPHEN RAND

Justice in Matthew's Gospel

'Let justice roll down like waters' (Amos 5:24, NRSV). Justice is a great theme of the Hebrew scriptures. God is 'just' and judges 'justly'. He calls his people to 'do justly', and the law given to Moses includes many instructions to deal fairly—with slaves, with aliens, and in business. The God of the Bible is a God of justice: 'Shall not the Judge of all the earth do right?' (Genesis 18:25, KJV).

So it's not surprising that Matthew's Gospel, the one that constantly echoes the Old Testament, should have divine and human justice as a major theme. It is not always in those words, because, in both Hebrew and Greek, the same words can be used for justice, judgement and righteousness. Justice establishes right principles, judgement decides what specific behaviour is right and wrong, and righteousness means actually doing it. As we shall see, Jesus encompasses all of those ideas, in both his teaching and his example. He proclaims the justice of God, he gives his followers the tools to decide for themselves what is right and wrong, and he calls people to seek 'God's kingdom and his righteousness' while exemplifying it in his own life.

Much of what Jesus has to say about justice in this Gospel is in story form—parables, as they are called. Bosses and workers, debtors and lenders, critics and their victims: the parade is colourful, sometimes stark. Each story makes a point, usually about what we would call being 'fair'. Justice and mercy both figure prominently.

Matthew's Gospel certainly encompasses this wonderful paradox of justice and mercy. The cross of Jesus with which it ends prefigures the vision of Revelation, where the one who sits on the throne (4:2), the eternal seat of judgement, is flanked by the Lamb who has been slain (5:6), the 'Lamb of God who takes away the sin of the world' (John 1:29, NRSV). There is the paradox in a picture. Perfect justice and perfect mercy exist alongside each other, both fulfilling the divine will, not in conflict but in a mutual purpose of salvation.

As we turn now to Matthew's Gospel, we shall constantly find the same glorious paradox—justice and judgement, yes, but also mercy and compassion.

DAVID WINTER

Only one judge

'Do not judge, so that you may not be judged. For with the judgement you make you will be judged, and the measure you give will be the measure you get. Why do you see the speck in your neighbour's eye, but do not notice the log in your own eye? Or how can you say to your neighbour, "Let me take the speck out of your eye", while the log is in your own eye? You hypocrite, first take the log out of your own eye, and then you will see clearly to take the speck out of your neighbour's eye.'

Here, Jesus the great teacher employs both gentle humour and sharp irony to make his point. The crowd would probably have laughed aloud as he described a man with a log in his eye offering to remove a speck of dust from someone else's. At the very least, the log would get in the way! But their laughter might have died away when they got the point. *They* were the man with the log in his eye. The neighbour they were so quick to judge was the one with the mere speck in his. A 'hypocrite' is an actor playing a part. What Jesus wants from us is reality.

We are always quick to see our own faults in others, though often we may not recognise them for what they are. The message of the rabbi Jesus was clear: 'Do not judge, so that you may not be judged' (v. 1). There can't be many of us who haven't struggled with this warning at times. Our churches are full of hasty judgements and self-righteous criticism. Even a friendly chat over a cup of tea can become a judgement session (about the vicar, parents with noisy children, what people wear in church, and so on). The message of Jesus is clear: the only judgement we are called to make is of our own behaviour. Everyone else's is the concern of the divine Judge.

Lord, help me to look first in the mirror at myself, before I look through the window at anyone else.

DAVID WINTER

Wilful blindness

'Woe to you, Chorazin! Woe to you, Bethsaida! For if the deeds of power done in you had been done in Tyre and Sidon, they would have repented long ago in sackcloth and ashes... And you, Capernaum, will you be exalted to heaven? No, you will be brought down to Hades. For if the deeds of power done in you had been done in Sodom, it would have remained until this day. But I tell you that on the day of judgement it will be more tolerable for the land of Sodom than for you.'

A figure of speech that Jesus frequently used in his teaching was hyperbole—obvious exaggeration to emphasise a point. It's common in our everyday language: we say, 'I could eat a horse' when what we would really like is a small cheese sandwich. Jesus used it a lot in his Sermon on the Mount, saying, for example, 'If your right eye causes you to sin, tear it out' (Matthew 5:29). Here he uses it to make the point that true judgement takes into account all the circumstances.

Jesus takes two extreme examples, and all his listeners would have recognised them both. One was the notorious city of Sodom (which abused Lot's family in defiance of every custom of hospitality at the time) and the other the Galilean town of Capernaum, which was the centre of the ministry of Jesus and the site of many of his miracles.

The crowd listening to Jesus would have assumed that Sodom, where this dreadful sexual violence took place against Abraham's relatives, was in line for fearful judgement, while beautiful Capernaum, nestling by the shore of the lake, would be honoured by the mighty acts of power done there by Jesus. But no, says Jesus. Think about it. Sodom knew nothing of the God of Israel and his commandments. What the people there did was utterly wrong, but they knew no better. Capernaum, on the other hand, saw the miracles and heard the teaching of Jesus but went on living as though they had neither seen nor heard. Sodom's failure was ignorance; Capernaum's was wilful blindness.

Sin is knowing what is wrong but still doing it. I suspect we've all been there. Thank God for forgiveness!

DAVID WINTER

Gentle justice

This was to fulfil what had been spoken by the prophet Isaiah: 'Here is my servant, whom I have chosen, my beloved, with whom my soul is well pleased. I will put my Spirit upon him, and he will proclaim justice to the Gentiles. He will not wrangle or cry aloud, nor will anyone hear his voice in the streets. He will not break a bruised reed or quench a smouldering wick until he brings justice to victory. And in his name the Gentiles will hope.'

Matthew has been describing the nature of the ministry of Jesus—especially his healing ministry. Here he uses some lines from one of the Servant Songs in Isaiah (42:1–4) to explain what the disciples were seeing of Jesus day by day. These precise words are not to be found in any recognised translation of Isaiah; Matthew is offering his own 'translation' of them. The great theme of Isaiah's words, however, is powerfully applied to what the disciples were seeing and hearing.

The emphasis is not so much on power (although Jesus' healing miracles were clearly mighty acts of power) but on gentleness. Unlike other would-be messiahs, Jesus didn't shout or dispute, but demonstrated his authority by extending the mercy and grace of God to the 'bruised reeds' (those bearing the injuries and hurts of life) and the 'smouldering wicks' (those whose hope was on the verge of dying out).

According to these words, the true Messiah's great passion will be justice. The Hebrew scriptures generally assumed that the Messiah would bring in a reign of justice in Israel, but Isaiah's 'Servant of the Lord' will proclaim worldwide justice ('justice to the Gentiles'). The kingdom of heaven will bring in a reign of justice for the whole world. The opening lines of this passage echo events at the baptism of Jesus (Matthew 3:17). Here, the 'beloved Son', empowered by the Spirit, proclaims the gentle justice of the new kingdom that he has come to inaugurate.

Most of us will sometimes have felt like 'bruised reeds', battered by circumstances, or 'smouldering wicks', near the end of our capacity to keep the flame of faith burning. The justice of Jesus has not come to break the weak or extinguish hope, but to restore hope and relight the flame of faith.

DAVID WINTER

Corrupt judgement

'Every kingdom divided against itself is laid waste, and no city or house divided against itself will stand. If Satan casts out Satan, he is divided against himself; how then will his kingdom stand? If I cast out demons by Beelzebul, by whom do your own exorcists cast them out? Therefore they will be your judges. But if it is by the Spirit of God that I cast out demons, then the kingdom of God has come to you.'

Jesus is here refuting a seriously offensive criticism, made by some of his detractors, that the power he has over all kinds of evil and darkness is not from God but from Satan, the very embodiment of all evil. ('Beelzebul' was one of the titles given to Satan.) Jesus refutes their argument with a piece of fairly obvious logic. If Satan is using Jesus to cast out Satan, what's the point of that? Is he fighting himself?

Jesus then makes a more powerful point. The healing ministry of Jesus represented the good, the whole and the healthy defeating the evil, the corrupt and the degrading. 'Demons' in New Testament thinking are the agents of confusion, the instruments of evil. Jesus came to deliver humanity from those things. So he sums it up in one sentence of ringing authority: 'If it is by the Spirit of God that I cast out demons, then the kingdom of God has come to you' (v. 28). The Pharisees, faced with the evidence of divine power, can only seek for other and more sinister explanations. If the Spirit of God is not doing it, then it must be done by the ultimate spirit of evil.

They are, Jesus tells them, in the presence of the 'kingdom of God'. This is an awesome moment of challenge. What they have seen, but refuse to recognise, is the very act of God himself, who alone can defeat the ultimate powers of evil. His 'kingdom has come' to them, bringing blessing to many but judgement to those who cannot or will not recognise the difference between what is good and holy and what is corrupt and evil.

Jesus is the light of the world. The light shines in the darkness, but it has to be recognised for what it is.

DAVID WINTER

Justice in the church

'If another member of the church sins against you, go and point out the fault when the two of you are alone. If the member listens to you, you have regained that one. But if you are not listened to, take one or two others along with you, so that every word may be confirmed by the evidence of two or three witnesses. If the member refuses to listen to them, tell it to the church; and if the offender refuses to listen even to the church, let such a one be to you as a Gentile and a tax collector.'

There are two problems with this passage to deal with first. 'Church' here isn't the one you go to each Sunday. That didn't exist when Jesus spoke these words. This 'church' (*ecclesia*) is simply a gathering or assembly, and the word was used to describe, among other things, the gathered people of Israel. Jesus obviously had in mind here his disciples, the 'gathering' of believers who would, after Pentecost, begin to form the Church, the body of Christ, as we know it. This, then, is the Church seen not as an organisation but as a living community of faith.

The second problem is about 'sins'. What is under consideration here is the spiritual well-being of a fellow disciple, not the application of church rules. It is the same kind of concern that Paul mentions in Colossians 3:16, where he urges the Christians, among other things, to 'admonish one another'. James 5:15 speaks of our prayers helping those who have sinned to find forgiveness. This is not being 'holier-than-thou' or accusing people of breaking church rules, but is an exercise of caring love—a desire to 'regain' one who may otherwise fall away. The process set out in Matthew's Gospel shares the hallmarks of Jewish justice: first, private; then limited; then the regulation 'three witnesses'. Only after that should the whole membership be involved.

Lord, let me tread very carefully, prayerfully and gently in my desire to help a fellow disciple who I think is going astray. Love, as so often, is the test.

DAVID WINTER

'As we forgive...'

'The kingdom of heaven may be compared to a king who wished to settle accounts with his slaves. When he began the reckoning, one who owed him ten thousand talents was brought to him; and, as he could not pay, his lord ordered him to be sold, together with his wife and children and all his possessions, and payment to be made. So the slave fell on his knees before him, saying, "Have patience with me, and I will pay you everything." And out of pity for him, the lord of that slave released him and forgave him the debt. But that same slave, as he went out, came upon one of his fellow slaves who owed him a hundred denarii; and seizing him by the throat, he said, "Pay what you owe." Then his fellow slave fell down and pleaded with him, "Have patience with me, and I will pay you." But he refused; then he went and threw him into prison until he should pay the debt.'

Tell this parable to a group of seven-year-olds and they will burst with indignation: 'It's not fair!' It certainly wasn't, when a man who had been let off a massive debt (about 15 years' wages) immediately demanded that one of his fellow slaves should instantly repay him a much smaller debt (about 100 days' wages). If you read the rest of the story, the first slave didn't get away with it. He ended up in prison until his whole debt was settled. Justice, in a sense, was done.

Yet this parable isn't really about justice; it's about forgiveness. Not an earthly lord, but almighty God, has forgiven us a lifetime of sins for the sake of his Son. How, given that, can we find it so difficult to forgive our fellow Christians (let alone everyone else) for their sins? It's there in the Lord's Prayer (which actually says 'debts' in Matthew's version, 6:12) and throughout the teaching of the New Testament. How can we miss it?

Those who forgive are forgiven. That's the simple formula.

DAVID WINTER

Generous justice

'When they received [the daily wage] they grumbled against the landowner, saying, "These last worked only one hour, and you have made them equal to us who have borne the burden of the day and the scorching heat." But he replied to one of them, "Friend, I am doing you no wrong; did you not agree with me for the usual daily wage? Take what belongs to you and go; I choose to give to this last the same as I give to you. Am I not allowed to do what I choose with what belongs to me? Or are you envious because I am generous?"'

This is the last part of the parable Jesus told about the hiring of workers in a vineyard. Workers would gather in the morning at the farm gates in the hope of being taken on for the day. In this case, the owner recruited some in the morning and then added others later in the day. When it came to pay time, those who had worked all day were indignant that the late recruits got exactly the same pay as they did. Today's passage is the response of the landowner.

What follows is a little essay in distinctions. The day-long workers were claiming that it was not fair that they should work all those hours for the same pay as the workers who had just popped in at the end. I think we could call that logical justice, and I suspect that any trade union would back their protest. What the landowner was talking about, though, was gracious justice. The workers' complaints stemmed from envy. The landowner wanted to be generous, but the stark logic of the day-long workers saw his generosity as preferential treatment. Once again the cry goes up, 'It's not fair!'

This is a parable of the kingdom of heaven, of course. Some will enjoy a lifetime of grace, blessing and discipleship. Others may come to them later in life, or even on their deathbed. But for everybody the reward is the same—eternal life.

God's generous justice does not work by mathematical logic but by love.

DAVID WINTER

Judgement justified

'Finally he sent his son to them, saying, "They will respect my son." But when the tenants saw the son, they said to themselves, "This is the heir; come, let us kill him and get his inheritance." So they seized him, threw him out of the vineyard, and killed him. Now when the owner of the vineyard comes, what will he do to those tenants?' They said to him, 'He will put those wretches to a miserable death, and lease the vineyard to other tenants who will give him the produce at the harvest time.'

This is the third of a series of parables that New Testament scholars call 'polemical': they are strongly worded attacks. The language is uncompromising. It speaks of irreversible decisions and their consequences. The historical background is the long and bitter controversy between the Christian Church (the 'new Israel', as the Christians saw themselves) and the 'old' Israel, whose leaders had rejected Jesus as Messiah.

The parable tells of a vineyard (an image of Israel) whose 'tenants' reject the rule of their master, the landowner, and even eventually kill his son. Some of the details of the story may stem from the Gospel writer's desire to interpret the parable for a later and wider Christian audience. As we find it in Matthew, the judgement is absolute and final. The leaders of Israel have wilfully and cruelly rejected the Son whom God sent. That decision, like all decisions, has had consequences. The bystanders listening to Jesus certainly got the point, though perhaps not seeing its immediate relevance to their own society.

But is this story only about the Jewish people of the first century? Certainly not. It is a warning that even in the regime of a loving and generous God (the vineyard owner who tried everything possible to preserve his precious vineyard), our decisions have inevitable consequences.

Despite all these problems, at the end there is still a vineyard, there are still tenants, and there is still fruit.

DAVID WINTER

Welcoming the 'others'

'Then [the king] said to his slaves, ' The wedding is ready, but those invited were not worthy. Go therefore into the main streets, and invite everyone you find to the wedding banquet." Those slaves went out into the streets and gathered all whom they found, both good and bad, so the wedding hall was filled with guests.'

This is one of several parables recorded by Matthew about the contemporary Jewish leaders' rejection of their Messiah, Jesus. The language, colourful and violent, is as uncompromising as in yesterday's reading. Those who make light of the invitation to the wedding banquet of the Messiah (a familiar prospect to those who knew the Hebrew scriptures) will be summarily rejected. Instead, the messianic blessings (a seat at the banquet) will be made open to everyone. Like the first Christian evangelists, sent out to 'make disciples of every nation', the king's servants will scour the highways and byways and urge people—whatever their background—to take a seat at the feast.

The whole story is worth reading, because the last part explains that it is not totally 'open house'. All are welcome (as the invitation in Revelation 22:17 puts it, 'Let anyone who wishes take the water of life'), but those who come must understand the etiquette of grace. The man without the wedding garment has simply declined to put on the proffered robe. The gift must be accepted and the grace received.

For the Jews of the time, this was a harsh indictment, and the early Church, which received the Gospels, was inclined to say, 'Serves them right.' That was not, however, how Paul saw it, longing that his fellow-Jews might share in Christ's salvation (Romans 9:1–5).

In the mysterious purposes of God, it was the rejection of the Messiah by the Jews that led, as God had promised Abraham, to 'all the nations of the earth' being blessed (Genesis 22:18). In the end, of course, that includes the people of the first covenant as well as of the new one. All are welcome, if they put on the free robe of grace.

DAVID WINTER

More than keeping rules

'Woe to you, scribes and Pharisees, hypocrites! For you clean the outside of the cup and of the plate, but inside they are full of greed and self-indulgence. You blind Pharisee! First clean the inside of the cup, so that the outside also may become clean. Woe to you, scribes and Pharisees, hypocrites! For you are like whitewashed tombs, which on the outside look beautiful, but inside they are full of the bones of the dead and of all kinds of filth.'

The most severe criticism to come from the lips of Jesus was not directed at the obvious targets—the swindling tax collectors, the thieves or the adulterers—but the most meticulously religious people of his day, the Pharisees. There were good Pharisees, as the Gospels acknowledge, but Jesus had nothing but scorn for those who elevated the keeping of obscure religious rules, about tithing mint and endless ritual washings, above generosity and kindness. The distinction he makes here is part of the experience of every religious person—inward or outward righteousness, expressed in the vivid picture of 'whitewashed tombs'.

We all know the dangers of public observance but private indulgence. Not many of us would fail to recognise that, too often, our secret private lives don't match our outward profession. Outside, the cup looks clean, but inwardly it still needs some more washing. Greed and self-indulgence are not limited to the Pharisees of the first century; nor are pride, envy and hypocrisy. We all know that a godly front can mask some pretty ungodly thoughts and actions. That is why there is a healthy honesty in the practice of regular confession of our sins, whether in church or at the close of day. I can remember the advice at my confirmation classes ages ago: 'Keep short accounts with God.' In doing so, we recognise what we would sooner ignore: as 1 John 1:8 puts it, 'If we say that we have no sin, we deceive ourselves.' Yet sin confessed, John's next verse tells us, is sin forgiven.

Lord, help me to see the bit of 'pharisee' that's in me, to repent of it and ask to be made inwardly clean.

DAVID WINTER

Sheep and goats

'When the Son of Man comes in his glory, and all the angels with him, then he will sit on the throne of his glory. All the nations will be gathered before him, and he will separate people one from another as a shepherd separates the sheep from the goats, and he will put the sheep at his right hand and the goats at the left. Then the king will say to those at his right hand, "Come, you that are blessed by my Father, inherit the kingdom prepared for you from the foundation of the world; for I was hungry and you gave me food, I was thirsty and you gave me something to drink, I was a stranger and you welcomed me, I was naked and you gave me clothing, I was sick and you took care of me, I was in prison and you visited me."'

This is part of the second of two parables about judgement. The first (Matthew 25:14–30) concerns the judgement of the lord's servants (the disciples—Christians, we may say). That is the story of the talents. You've been given grace, so what have you done with it? The one that follows it is about the judgement of the 'nations'—that is, everybody else. When Jesus comes as judge of the whole world, how will he go about his work?

Well, it will be like a shepherd separating sheep from goats, but the test Jesus will apply is not what they look like but what they have done, and specifically how they have treated the 'members of his family' (v. 40). What they do to his disciples, he explains, they are doing to him, whether it's generosity and kindness, or rejection.

So the first parable does not contradict the fundamental Christian truth that we are saved by faith through grace, and the second parable offers an invitation to the people of the 'nations' to treat the followers of Jesus as though they were the Saviour himself. I suppose, really, it's an invitation to respond as positively as possible to any contact they may have with the people and message of his good news.

We are not saved by our good works. Our good works are the evidence that we are saved.

DAVID WINTER

Justice denied

So when Pilate saw that he could do nothing, but rather that a riot was beginning, he took some water and washed his hands before the crowd, saying, 'I am innocent of this man's blood; see to it yourselves.' Then the people as a whole answered, 'His blood be on us and on our children!' So he released Barabbas for them; and after flogging Jesus, he handed him over to be crucified.

The historical background is very important in interpreting this passage. Roman records tell us that Pontius Pilate was a weak and impulsive prefect of Judea who came into the post in AD26 with a record of antisemitic connections in Rome. A few years after the crucifixion, he was summoned to Rome to answer charges of cruelty in Samaria, so the impression we might get from the Gospels of a man who stood for justice and law, against the Jewish crowd, perhaps owes more to later interpretation of the events. 'His blood be on us' was exactly how the early church interpreted the plight of the Jews after the destruction of Jerusalem in AD70. Partly because Pilate despised the chief priests, he was unwilling to take the responsibility that was clearly and undeniably his, not the crowd's, for the judgement of Jesus.

The gesture of washing his hands of responsibility was pointless. He *was* responsible. Jesus could not have been executed without his permission, or at least connivance. He was commander of the army, and it was his soldiers who crucified Jesus. However much he tried, he could not be 'innocent of the blood of this just man' (as many early manuscripts report his words). Like so many, Pilate had power but ducked responsibility. So the only completely innocent person in the whole world was taken away to be crucified. It wasn't the first massive miscarriage of justice in history, nor, by a long way, the last—but it was certainly the most momentous.

We all have responsibilities—as parents, grandparents, friends, teachers and neighbours. 'Washing our hands' won't do. Accepting responsibility is a Christian duty.

DAVID WINTER

An onlooker's judgement

Then Jesus cried again with a loud voice and breathed his last. At that moment the curtain of the temple was torn in two, from top to bottom. The earth shook, and the rocks were split... Now when the centurion and those with him, who were keeping watch over Jesus, saw the earthquake and what took place, they were terrified and said, 'Truly this man was God's Son!'

These are the last moments of the earthly life of Jesus. He 'breathed his last'. Breath, in biblical terms, is the life-giving gift of God and at this moment the body of the Son of God surrendered it. Thus the sacrifice was made—the one perfect sacrifice for sins, for ever. The watching crowds were silenced. The execution party, hardbitten Roman soldiers, stood there and watched in perplexity as darkness fell and the earth trembled. What was happening? Then their officer, the centurion whose duty it had been to stand before the cross and watch the prisoner die, uttered his own verdict: 'Truly this man was God's Son!'

He didn't, of course, mean by those words what Christians believe— that Jesus is divine, sharing God's very nature. For a Roman, a 'son of God' (which is how the NRSV footnote renders his words) is a person of absolute righteousness. The centurion had watched Jesus on the cross, heard the words he spoke, seen both his dignity in the face of insult and abuse and his compassion ('Father, forgive them', Luke 23:34). This was not how Pilate or the scornful members of the crowd saw him; it was what we might call a neutral observer's verdict. Everything about this man cried out that he was good, and good in a special way.

As Jesus died, the Gospels record, the 'curtain of the temple was torn in two, from top to bottom' (v. 51). Perhaps it was a result of the earthquake, but, whatever its cause, the message is clear. Everything has changed. The old order has passed. There is no longer a need for high priests and animal sacrifices. The way to God is open for all who seek it, even an exhausted Roman centurion.

The broken body on the cross proclaims a wonderful truth. God is good, this is how much he loves us—and this is his beloved Son.

DAVID WINTER

All authority, all nations, all the way

Now the eleven disciples went to Galilee, to the mountain to which Jesus had directed them... And Jesus came and said to them, 'All authority in heaven and on earth has been given to me. Go therefore and make disciples of all nations, baptising them in the name of the Father and of the Son and of the Holy Spirit, and teaching them to obey everything that I have commanded you. And remember, I am with you always, to the end of the age.'

This is what we call the 'great commission', the charge that Jesus gave to the eleven remaining apostles, which, by transmission, becomes the charter for his Church for the whole of time. One key word in this passage is 'therefore' (v. 19): because Jesus has 'all authority', it is not presumptuous of the apostles to go to every nation and turn seekers into disciples, or to require those disciples to live in line with his teaching and example.

The other key word is 'authority' (v. 18). The King James Bible says 'All power', but 'authority' conveys the meaning more precisely. There are two words in the New Testament that can be translated 'power'. One (the root of our word 'dynamic') means the sheer ability to get things done. Jesus showed that power in his mighty acts. The other word, the one used here, means 'authority' in the sense of the judicial right to bring something about. The Son of God had received that authority from his Father, and was now passing it on to his disciples.

Justice, our theme for these readings, depends in the end on the existence of an absolute authority, which can say, 'This is right, and that is wrong.' Only God himself can speak with that final authority. 'Righteousness and justice are the foundation of your throne,' says Psalm 89:14. Now these disciples are to be the foundation of the new community of the baptised.

Living under the authority of Jesus—his teaching, his example—is possible only because he has promised to be with us 'all the way' (the literal translation of the final verse). All authority, all nations, all the way!

DAVID WINTER

Peace in Romans

Whether email or handwritten letters, our correspondence can be divided into two categories. Some messages have a familiar tone. They show signs of acquaintance with the recipients' circumstances. The style and content suggest a degree of shared history. Others show no hint of prior relationship. These more formal messages tend to be carefully structured rather than chatty. Within the collection of Paul's letters in our Bibles, Romans is set apart by its character and substance.

Paul's letters comprise a treasure trove of theological insight, pastoral astuteness and practical wisdom. In many cases, Paul had helped to establish the congregations with whom he corresponded. He wrote to encourage them in their trials and challenge them over particular problems. Warm individual greetings and specific details characterise these letters; they are personal follow-ups with people in whom he had already made considerable investment in labour and prayer. However, his letter to 'all in Rome who are loved by God and called to be his holy people' (Romans 1:7) is directed to Christians in a place where he had not set foot.

Paul's lack of personal connection with Rome, his intense desire to visit and his strong concern for the Romans' spiritual development combine to make this letter distinctive. It is a carefully crafted exposition of the gospel, a kind of Christian manifesto. In health care, many medicines are designed to treat particular illnesses, but others are 'prophylactic'—preventative measures. Most of Paul's letters deal with specific concerns about matters as diverse as false teaching, abuse of power and personal conflict, but Romans is 'prophylactic', aiming to prevent difficulties through a right understanding of the gospel and by anticipating questions.

The key topics of this most tremendous explanation of the gospel are numerous, but we are going to focus on the single, crucial theme of peace. Like examining the many facets of a well-cut diamond, we shall reflect on peace from the various viewpoints that Paul's letter affords. Passages explaining the means of peace between humankind and God form the backbone of his teaching. In Paul's understanding, this reconciliation between the Creator and his people then leads to peace between God's people—a revolution in relationships, in which divisions dissolve.

STEVE AISTHORPE

The God of peace

The God of peace be with you all... Now may the God of peace, who through the blood of the eternal covenant brought back from the dead our Lord Jesus, that great Shepherd of the sheep, equip you with everything good for doing his will, and may he work in us what is pleasing to him, through Jesus Christ, to whom be glory for ever and ever.

In the 2003 film *Bruce Almighty*, Jim Carrey plays Bruce, a disillusioned TV reporter with a distorted view of God. In one outburst he cries out, 'Oh God, why do you hate me? God is a kid sitting on an ant-hill with a magnifying glass—and I'm that ant.' Bruce's warped view leads him to accuse God of not doing his job properly, and God responds by giving Bruce the opportunity to try the role himself. It makes for good entertainment but also makes an important point: our vision of God has a profound impact on how we understand everything else. It shapes us and the way we live.

Of course, this side of eternity we will never have a complete understanding of the glorious, multifaceted character of God. There will always be a degree of mystery. However, as we pray, as we assimilate the strands of truth available to us and as we seek to unlearn the inaccurate impressions we become aware of, so we grow into greater truth and are changed in the process.

For Paul, there were certain aspects of the divine character about which he was utterly confident. Based on his intimate knowledge of the Hebrew scriptures and his own experience, he knew for sure that his Creator and Saviour was none other than 'the God of peace'—an assurance shared by the writer of the letter to the Hebrews.

In common parlance, 'peace' has come to mean an absence of conflict or a feeling of calm. However, for Paul, 'peace' denoted the Hebrew concept of *shalom*, a person's highest good and deepest well-being. His understanding of salvation and every aspect of Christian living was shaped by his knowledge of God as the source of all peace. The peace he writes of is the origin and consequence of right relationships in every sphere of life.

Know for sure that our God is 'the God of peace'.

STEVE AISTHORPE

A profound blessing

Through him we received grace and apostleship to call all the Gentiles to the obedience that comes from faith for his name's sake. And you also are among those Gentiles who are called to belong to Jesus Christ. To all in Rome who are loved by God and called to be his holy people: Grace and peace to you from God our Father and from the Lord Jesus Christ.

The first time we meet Paul face to face, he is on the road to Damascus (Acts 9:1–2). The account of that journey has a contemporary ring to it, for all the wrong reasons, because here is a religious extremist on his way to Syria, intent on the violent persecution of believers.

It is good to remind ourselves that the apostle who writes 'grace and peace' (v. 7) to the followers of Christ in Rome is the same person who, some years previously, was 'breathing out murderous threats against the Lord's disciples' (Acts 9:1). Paul became such a powerful advocate for God's grace and peace precisely because he himself was so utterly transformed by that same grace and peace.

Grace makes the gift of forgiveness possible. It speaks of the deepest love imaginable, a love that is able to offer forgiveness freely because it has been paid for entirely by another. On the cross of Christ, Paul's vast debt was fully paid, his guilt erased. Grace enabled this vicious terrorist not only to be free from the consequences of his wrongdoing, but also to enter into a relationship of *shalom*, peace, with the God and with the people against whom he had railed.

It could be argued that the phrase 'grace and peace' forms the most succinct summary of this whole epistle. No doubt, for Paul, the phrase 'grace and peace' also contained echoes of the poetic beauty and theological enormity of the blessing that Yahweh gave to Moses, to enable Aaron and his descendants to bless God's people: 'The Lord bless you and keep you; the Lord make his face shine on you and be gracious to you; the Lord turn his face toward you and give you peace' (Numbers 6:24–26).

Pray a blessing on your neighbours, your family, the people you find difficult and, finally, yourself: 'Grace and peace.'

STEVE AISTHORPE

The need for peace

As it is written: 'There is no one righteous, not even one; there is no one who understands; there is no one who seeks God. All have turned away, they have together become worthless; there is no one who does good, not even one.' 'Their throats are open graves; their tongues practise deceit.' 'The poison of vipers is on their lips.' 'Their mouths are full of cursing and bitterness.' 'Their feet are swift to shed blood; ruin and misery mark their ways, and the way of peace they do not know.' 'There is no fear of God before their eyes.'

In September 1938, British Prime Minister Neville Chamberlain returned from a visit to Germany and declared that he and Adolf Hitler had signed a joint declaration which promised, he assured his listeners, 'peace for our time'. Within a year, the two countries were at war.

We all long for peace. It is tempting for our politicians to promise it. Sadly, such undertakings often mirror the words of Jeremiah, criticising the leaders of his day: '"Peace, peace," they say, when there is no peace' (Jeremiah 6:14). Some of us are blessed to live in what we consider peaceful countries. However, even if conflict is not a feature of daily life, there is much that is contrary to the kind of peace expressed by *shalom*, the ultimate expression of well-being and love-based relationships.

Occasionally Paul treats his readers to a style of argument he learned from his rabbis: a series of quotations from the scriptures, known as *charaz*, literally 'a string of pearls'. In today's reading he amasses passages from the Psalms and Isaiah to drive home his point that, without reverence for God, there is no peace. Together these verses comprise a litany of human depravity. If there is any uncertainty regarding the all-pervasive nature of human rebellion and the seriousness of the resultant predicament, his repetition of 'no one', 'not even one', 'no one', 'no one' (vv. 10–11) removes any shred of doubt. In such a state, 'the way of peace' (v. 17; Isaiah 59:8) is unknown.

The discovery of peace becomes possible when we recognise its absence and the futility of following our natural inclinations as a means of pursuing it.

STEVE AISTHORPE

Peace with God

Therefore, since we have been justified through faith, we have peace with God through our Lord Jesus Christ, through whom we have gained access by faith into this grace in which we now stand. And we boast in the hope of the glory of God. Not only so, but we also glory in our sufferings, because we know that suffering produces perseverance; perseverance, character; and character, hope. And hope does not put us to shame, because God's love has been poured out into our hearts through the Holy Spirit, who has been given to us.

This is one of Paul's great outpourings of sheer wonder. Reflecting on the astonishing gift and privilege of 'peace with God' (v. 1) and all that flows from it, he breaks forth into a rhapsody of gratitude and awe. This peace cannot be bought or earned, but is available 'through faith' and 'through our Lord Jesus Christ'.

There is a famous picture of President J.F. Kennedy in the Oval Office of the White House with his son, John Jr, playing under his desk. The charm of the picture stems from the way it brings together the most powerful man on earth, sitting in the place that symbolises great authority, with the simple, trusting play of a child. Others would only ever enter that space (and never play in it!) by special authorisation, but John Jr was there because the commander-in-chief was his dad.

The phrase 'gained access by' (v. 2) translates a word that was used in the context of ushering someone into the royal court. It implies the granting of access to the most privileged position, the 'bringing near' of someone to a person of greatness. The peace offered by our gracious God extends beyond forgiveness. As Jesus died, 'the curtain of the temple was torn in two' (Matthew 27:51); the barrier guarding the Most Holy Place was ripped 'top to bottom'. We are permanently welcome in the royal court.

In this we gain a foretaste of glory—a glimpse that transforms our perspective on any suffering. Adversity is temporary and trivial compared with the glory to come, and has a purpose in God's shaping of our character.

The King of kings welcomes you into his presence.

STEVE AISTHORPE

Peace for all

Where, then, is boasting? It is excluded. Because of what law? The law that requires works? No, because of the 'law' that requires faith. For we maintain that a person is justified by faith apart from the works of the law. Or is God the God of Jews only? Is he not the God of Gentiles too? Yes, of Gentiles too, since there is only one God, who will justify the circumcised by faith and the uncircumcised through that same faith. Do we, then, nullify the law by this faith? Not at all! Rather, we uphold the law.

Paul was tutored by Gamaliel, the preeminent teacher of his day (Acts 5:34). He knew the scriptures inside out. Although he did not recognise Jesus as the Messiah immediately, when he did he had an outstanding overview of God's plans as revealed through the law and prophets. In particular, Paul realised, in calling Israel, God always intended that 'all peoples on earth' would be blessed through them (Genesis 12:2–3).

From our perspective, with two millennia of hindsight, the proclamation that, in Christ, peace with God is for Jews and Gentiles alike seems unremarkable. However, for his original readers, Paul's insistence that peace with God led to peace with one another was radical and controversial. For Jews, it raised the pressing questions that Paul pre-empts as he writes to Rome. In this epistle Paul explains in forensic detail the theological reasoning undergirding the truth summarised in the statement 'You are all one in Christ Jesus' (Galatians 3:28). Regardless of race, gender or any other distinction, peace with God comes 'by faith' (Romans 3:30), and that brings with it fellowship with all believers.

The moment we recognise God as 'Abba, Father' (Romans 8:15), we inherit a multitude of siblings. The plethora of church denominations sometimes mask the truth that, ultimately, we are members of one Church. Diversity will always prevail and should be celebrated; we will continue to be people of different nations, tribes and languages (Revelation 7:9). However, peace is available for all and joins us into one family.

Allow this truth to guide your prayers today: 'In Christ we, though many, form one body, and each member belongs to all the others' (Romans 12:5).

STEVE AISTHORPE

A fruitful peace

God 'will repay each person according to what they have done.' To those who by persistence in doing good seek glory, honour and immortality, he will give eternal life. But for those who are self-seeking and who reject the truth and follow evil, there will be wrath and anger. There will be trouble and distress for every human being who does evil: first for the Jew, then for the Gentile; but glory, honour and peace for everyone who does good: first for the Jew, then for the Gentile. For God does not show favouritism.

Can this be the same Paul who wrote, 'We maintain that a person is justified by faith' (3:28)? Is he contradicting himself? How are we to understand today's passage, which, taken on its own, seems to suggest that our status before God is determined by our actions? Here, 'peace' seems to be reserved for those who 'do good' (v. 10) and no mention is made of faith. Is Paul suggesting that instead of, or as well as, the glorious grace he celebrates elsewhere, there is some kind of cosmic karma at work? Is our eternal peace dependent on a scorecard of good deeds?

Be in no doubt: Paul is not one to contradict himself. In the opening verse of today's passage Paul quotes from Psalm 62:12 as one part of his explanation of 'the gospel… promised beforehand through his prophets in the Holy Scriptures' (Romans 1:2–3). When Jesus, with his final breath, uttered the word we translate as 'It is finished' (John 19:30), his meaning was clear and decisive. The word was used on receipts in the first century, meaning 'the debt is paid in full'; no further payment is required. The price of peace has been paid and is offered freely to 'all who believe' (Romans 3:22).

The consistent 'doing good' of which Paul speaks is not the cost of peace; it is the fruit. Peace with God is accompanied by a transformation, and our actions are the evidence of it. Authentic faith changes us. A living faith leads to a loving life.

Lord Jesus, thank you that you have paid the price of peace.
Inspire and energise me to live a life of 'doing good'.

STEVE AISTHORPE

The outgrowth of a Spirit-controlled mind

So I say, live by the Spirit, and you will not gratify the desires of the flesh. For the flesh desires what is contrary to the Spirit, and the Spirit what is contrary to the flesh... But the fruit of the Spirit is love, joy, peace, forbearance, kindness, goodness, faithfulness, gentleness and self-control. Against such things there is no law. Those who belong to Christ Jesus have crucified the flesh with its passions and desires. Since we live by the Spirit, let us keep in step with the Spirit.

Just when we think it cannot get any better, when it seems that Paul must have reached the heights in his explanation of all that has been made possible, he explains that God, having restored us into a harmonious relationship with himself, works to cultivate his character in us. 'He decided from the outset to shape the lives of those who love him along the same lines as the life of his Son' (Romans 8:29, *THE MESSAGE*). God is not merely patching things up with an insubordinate people; he is restoring the whole creation according to its original purpose—and we are part of the plan.

As the God of peace sets about renovating the lives of his people, with the 'Prince of peace' as a blueprint, it is not surprising that peace is among the characteristics that emerge. Allowing God's Spirit to direct our steps is a recipe for 'life and peace' (Romans 8:6).

But what does 'walking by the Spirit' mean in practice? Our days are filled with choices, some subconscious, others deliberate. Without conscious attention to our decisions and their implications, we sail through life driven by the winds of social trends, fads and fashions, the subliminal expectations of others, and our own unchecked desires. However, when we pray we press the pause button. When we request his direction and discernment, we permit, in the words of Paul, 'the peace of Christ' to be the umpire of our hearts (Colossians 3:15), allowing his peace to affirm or a lack of peace to challenge or warn us.

God of peace, as I seek to live a life guided by your peace,
please nurture within me the fruit of your Spirit which is peace.

STEVE AISTHORPE

Reconciliation

God demonstrates his own love for us in this: while we were still sinners, Christ died for us. Since we have now been justified by his blood, how much more shall we be saved from God's wrath through him! For if, while we were God's enemies, we were reconciled to him through the death of his Son, how much more, having been reconciled, shall we be saved through his life! Not only is this so, but we also boast in God through our Lord Jesus Christ, through whom we have now received reconciliation.

Recent decades have seen the words 'peace' and 'reconciliation' more frequently being spoken in the same breath. From South Africa to Rwanda and from the Balkans to Belfast, people have recognised that the ending of hostilities is the beginning of establishing restored relationships.

The fact that reconciliation is needed means that there was previously hostility, and, in human conflicts, the causes invariably have origins in all parties involved. However, the reconciliation that inspires Paul to brim over with gratitude is different in some important ways. First, while there was enmity between God and humankind, God never ceased to love us. Indeed, while we were still in active rebellion, his extravagant, unwarranted love led him to make the greatest sacrifice imaginable, in order to wage peace and lay foundations for reconciliation.

Also, while reconciliation requires the key grounds of enmity to be addressed, in the case of our broken relationship with our Creator, the wrong was genuinely all on one side. The holy character of God means that he abhors all that is evil and unjust. Our rebellious nature had to be dealt with. The Bible uses the word 'sin' to translate a number of different Hebrew and Greek terms, but they all have in common a mindset or actions that are 'hostile to God' (Romans 8:7).

Twice in today's passage Paul uses the phrase 'how much more' (vv. 9–10) to highlight that, while something truly remarkable has already happened, the implications for the future are more breathtaking still.

The death of Jesus has accomplished more than we can ever grasp; his resurrection life is achieving and will achieve yet more.

STEVE AISTHORPE

Abba, Father

The mind governed by the flesh is death, but the mind governed by the Spirit is life and peace… For those who are led by the Spirit of God are the children of God. The Spirit you received does not make you slaves, so that you live in fear again; rather, the Spirit you received brought about your adoption to sonship. And by him we cry, 'Abba, Father.' The Spirit himself testifies with our spirit that we are God's children.

The depth and extent and benefits of the astonishing peace that we have through the grace of God seem to know no bounds. Not only are we forgiven; not only are we welcomed into the presence of the king; we are now told that inherent to this peace is the intimacy and full inheritance rights of an adopted child. The same Spirit that gives us 'life and peace' (v. 6) generates within us an assurance so profound that it causes us to think of and address the almighty God in the most familiar terms. 'Abba' is the same Aramaic word for 'father' that we find on the lips of Jesus as he contemplates the horror of his impending death, in Gethsemane. For him, it also spoke of a robust confidence in God's sovereignty and unquestionable power: '"Abba, Father," he said, "everything is possible for you"' (Mark 14:36).

Paul is eager to emphasise that the comfort and confidence in the presence of God experienced by all who trust in Jesus are not just feelings. The term translated as 'adoption' (v. 15) had a specific legal and cultural meaning for his readers. To be 'adopted' in the Roman world meant that any rights or debts associated with pre-adoption life were erased completely and replaced with the full and unequivocal rights and responsibilities of inheritance in the new family. Adoption ceremonies were authenticated by witnesses. If, at a later date, there was any doubt as to the veracity or validity of the adoption, it was the role of the witnesses to speak up and confirm the truth. In the case of the Christian, 'the Spirit himself testifies with our spirit that we are God's children' (v. 16).

Abba, Father, thank you for the privilege of being adopted into your family.

STEVE MOTHURPE

Good news of peace

As Scripture says, 'Anyone who believes in him will never be put to shame.' For there is no difference between Jew and Gentile—the same Lord is Lord of all and richly blesses all who call on him, for, 'Everyone who calls on the name of the Lord will be saved.' How, then, can they call on the one they have not believed in? And how can they believe in the one of whom they have not heard? And how can they hear without someone preaching to them? And how can anyone preach unless they are sent? As it is written: 'How beautiful are the feet of those who bring good news!'

Paul's logic is faultless. He is a master of crafting and illustrating explanations. Working back from the need for people to call out to their Saviour, he highlights the importance of people who communicate 'the gospel of peace' (v. 15, KJV).

The terms 'preach' and 'preaching' here (vv. 14–15) must not be understood in the limited sense of religious leaders expounding a sermon. In Paul's mind was the role of the herald, a person who, before the days of printing presses or modern mass communication, delivered messages. Prior to other means of getting the word out, the role of faithful messengers was vital. If royal decrees and public declarations were to get beyond the royal chamber or governor's office, human messengers needed to be entrusted with their faithful delivery. So, when the news being conveyed was good news, the sight of the messenger was a delight: 'like a snow-cooled drink at harvest time' (Proverbs 25:13).

'How beautiful are the feet of those who bring good news of peace' (v. 15) was a phrase used by the prophet Isaiah, referring to the messengers who proclaimed the release of the exiles from captivity in Babylon (Isaiah 52:7)—and then by Nahum with reference to the deliverance of God's people from the Assyrians. These were, however, glimpses of the ultimate deliverance to come; they were examples of God's gracious intervention, foreshadowing the greater good news of peace of which Paul speaks.

Thank you, Lord, for faithful envoys of God's peace in every generation. Please enable me to be a reliable messenger of this good news.

STEVE AISTHORPE

Proactive peace-making

Do not repay anyone evil for evil. Be careful to do what is right in the eyes of everyone. If it is possible, as far as it depends on you, live at peace with everyone. Do not take revenge, my dear friends, but leave room for God's wrath, for it is written: 'It is mine to avenge; I will repay,' says the Lord. On the contrary: 'If your enemy is hungry, feed him; if he is thirsty, give him something to drink. In doing this, you will heap burning coals on his head.' Do not be overcome by evil, but overcome evil with good.

Having reminded his readers in the preceding verses of the importance of offering themselves wholeheartedly to God, having urged them to have a healthy perspective on themselves, and having encouraged them in their love for brothers and sisters in Christ, Paul now delivers an even more radical and demanding directive. While his practical instruction to serve enemies and do everything possible to be at peace with everyone was (and is) counter-cultural, it is entirely consistent with both the teaching and example of Jesus (Matthew 5:44).

However, Paul is realistic in his implication that peace is not always, or often, entirely in our hands. The nature of human relationships is that it is rarely within the power of any one person to resolve conflict or maintain peace. Paul's teaching is not only about responding with grace to enemies; it is not just an injunction against countering insult with insult, or violence with violence, or a ban on retaliation, reprisal or revenge. The Christian imperative is proactive peace-building. Followers of the Prince of peace are to be peacemakers; disciples of Christ are called to cultivate the habit of doing all possible, 'as far as it depends on you' (v. 18). We are to strive to 'overcome evil with good' (v. 21) and to make 'every effort to do what leads to peace' (Romans 14:19).

Bodies offered as 'living sacrifices' and minds 'renewed' by the trans-formational activity of God's Spirit (Romans 12:1–2) are a recipe for peacemakers, people who 'will be called children of God' (Matthew 5:9).

Make the prayer of St Francis a meditation and your heartfelt plea:
'Lord, make me a channel of your peace.'

STEVE AISTHORPE

A kingdom peace

I am convinced, being fully persuaded in the Lord Jesus, that nothing is unclean in itself. But if anyone regards something as unclean, then for that person it is unclean. If your brother or sister is distressed because of what you eat, you are no longer acting in love. Do not by your eating destroy someone for whom Christ died. Therefore do not let what you know is good be spoken of as evil. For the kingdom of God is not a matter of eating and drinking, but of righteousness, peace and joy in the Holy Spirit, because anyone who serves Christ in this way is pleasing to God and receives human approval. Let us therefore make every effort to do what leads to peace and to mutual edification.

Compared to the Gospel writers, Paul only rarely mentions the kingdom of God. This kingdom is unequivocally central to the teaching of Jesus. He insisted that the kingdom should be our highest priority (Matthew 6:33). He never gave a tidy definition of it, but his meaning was clear: 'Your kingdom come, your will be done, on earth as it is in heaven' (Matthew 6:10). So, does the fact that this letter to Rome, Paul's magnum opus, contains only the single reference (the one in today's reading) imply that the kingdom was unimportant in his understanding of the gospel?

Far from it! Rather, the few mentions in Paul's correspondence show that the kingdom was already familiar to and of central importance to Paul and his readers. By reminding Roman believers of the priority of the kingdom, he wanted to put other matters in right perspective. In particular, his concern was for Christians to prioritise the well-being of others before they considered their own preferences. Taking the example of eating and drinking, he pointed out that individual preferences or cultural norms regarding food and drink are inconsequential trivia when considered in the wider perspective of the kingdom. After all, the kingdom, the reign of Christ, did not come to them because of dietary habits.

Paul's recipe for 'peace and mutual edification' (v. 19) means deprioritising personal preferences and prioritising the good of others. Refocus on the kingdom—life under the rule of Jesus—characterised by 'righteousness, peace and joy in the Holy Spirit' (v. 18).

STEVE AISTHORPE

The presence of the God of peace

I urge you, brothers and sisters, by our Lord Jesus Christ and by the love of the Spirit, to join me in my struggle by praying to God for me. Pray that I may be kept safe from the unbelievers in Judea and that the contribution I take to Jerusalem may be favourably received by the Lord's people there, so that I may come to you with joy, by God's will, and in your company be refreshed. The God of peace be with you all. Amen.

Should a devoted follower of the one who taught that when we give, our giving should be 'in secret' (Matthew 6:3–4) really be so open about discussing the gift he is delivering to the central church? Throughout his correspondence, Paul celebrates the enthusiastic donations of recently established Gentile congregations: 'In the midst of a very severe trial, their overflowing joy and their extreme poverty welled up in rich generosity' (2 Corinthians 8:2). He pleaded with others to do likewise (1 Corinthians 16:1–4), and in the letter before us he appealed for prayer 'that the contribution I take to Jerusalem may be favourably received' (v. 31).

This collection was much more than a contribution to people in material need. The gift that Paul took to Jerusalem was a symbol of Gentile–Jewish solidarity at a time when the unity of the church was still being forged. How would this offering from fledgling Gentile churches be received? Paul's concern was not merely about whether the recipients would be offended by being seen as in need of charity; he was urging prayer for the unity and well-being of the body of Christ. The integrity of the church, the principle of 'all one in Christ', hung in the balance. Would the church be fragmented along racial lines or would it be a faithful sign of the kingdom to come?

Paul was fully aware of the hardships that awaited him in Jerusalem (Acts 24:17–18), but he was convinced that the God of peace was with him—and that was enough. When it came to praying for his brothers and sisters in Rome, he had no higher hope than that they too would know this awesome presence.

For whom might you pray today: 'The God of peace be with you'?

STEVE AISTHORPE

A decisive peace

I urge you, brothers and sisters, to watch out for those who cause divisions and put obstacles in your way that are contrary to the teaching you have learned. Keep away from them. For such people are not serving our Lord Christ, but their own appetites. By smooth talk and flattery they deceive the minds of naive people. Everyone has heard about your obedience, so I rejoice because of you; but I want you to be wise about what is good, and innocent about what is evil. The God of peace will soon crush Satan under your feet. The grace of our Lord Jesus be with you.

Paul's letter to the believers in Rome was written during a period described as *Pax Romana*, 'the Roman peace'. After centuries scarred by one violent conflict after another, fuelled by a voracious appetite for expansion, the might of Rome imposed an era devoid of war. Rather than being a time of harmony between the diverse peoples of the region, it was a 'peace' that resulted from having crushed all adversaries. However, if anyone were to understand 'peace' in terms of a quiet life and a lack of conflict, then to be a follower of Jesus Christ was definitely not a formula for achieving it.

To embrace the Christian faith in the first-century Roman empire was, for many people, to guarantee tribulations of the most brutal kind. To call Jesus 'Lord' was seen as an act of treason; only the emperor and the state-sponsored Roman gods of the day were deemed worthy of devotion, and rivalry was dealt with in ruthless fashion. Paul probably wrote his letter before Emperor Nero ordered the state-sponsored persecution of the Christian community (a decree that led to believers being torn apart by dogs and set on fire as 'human torches'), but a culture of contempt towards Christians, verging on hatred, was already fermenting.

So it was into this situation of unimaginable trials and understandable anxiety that Paul wrote the precious assurance that the final outcome of history is secure. Christ is the victor and, although hostility and evil persist for the time being, the kingdom of love and justice will triumph.

God of peace, thank you for the guarantee that you will prevail.

STEVE AISTHORPE

Praying Bible prayers

I have been told that there are some 650 prayers in the Bible, but that probably depends on how widely we define what constitutes a prayer. From my own rummaging in scripture I have compiled a list of about 80 prayers in which we are told exactly what was prayed—in other words, where we are given the content of the prayer.

Over the next two weeks we will look at a selection of these prayers, found in both Old and New Testaments. Prayer is a theme that runs throughout the Bible, seen not just in teaching about prayer and exhortations to pray, but in the actual practice of prayer as well. These ancient prayers can become a foundation for our own prayer life and so enrich our walk with God.

Many readers will be familiar with liturgical prayer and will know the benefit of using written prayers and of making the words their own. Why not, then, make the prayers of the Bible your own? This is what I hope will happen as, each day, we take a prayer from scripture, ponder its meaning and then use it in our own devotions.

Any selection like this will be highly subjective. For example, I have deliberately not included some of the longer prayers in the Bible, and have used only one prayer from the book of Psalms, although many are found there. I have also resisted the temptation (I think) of choosing my own favourite prayers, trying rather to sense which ones I should include to benefit my readers most. This has led me to some of the shorter, less well-known prayers. However, a certain flow has developed as one prayer leads into another, and I hope you will be able to feel it as you read.

Prayer is such a special gift to us—mysterious, certainly, and sometimes frustrating, yet always making the connection between God and his people alive and real. And the best way to understand prayer is simply… to pray.

TONY HORSFALL

A prayer for bringing up children

Then Manoah prayed to the Lord: 'Pardon your servant, Lord. I beg you to let the man of God you sent to us come again to teach us how to bring up the boy who is to be born.'

There is no doubt in my mind that the task of bringing up a family is one of the most challenging things we ever do, and it is getting harder all the time. All the more reason, therefore, to take note of this little-known prayer for help.

The child to be born in this case is Samson, one of the great characters in the Old Testament. His parents were unable to conceive and had probably given up hope of having a child. Then a mysterious stranger appeared to Manoah's wife, telling her that she would have a son who would be set apart for God and would deliver Israel from the Philistines. In answer to this specific prayer, the stranger returns and instructs them further. As they entertain him, they realise that he is the angel of the Lord and this has been a divine visitation.

Our most instinctive response to parenting is to duplicate the way in which we were parented ourselves. This may or may not be helpful, but either way there is always more we can learn about what it means to be a parent, and it is not a sign of failure or inadequacy to seek out help and advice from others with more experience. The Bible is full of parental wisdom; there are other helpful books we can read, courses to attend, and internet sites where we can research specific issues.

It is important that churches welcome and encourage those who are bringing up children—particularly single parents, those who foster, and those who have children with special needs. Sometimes, as we get older, we may forget how demanding parenthood is, and this can make us less than sympathetic towards those whose children appear disruptive. Why not pause and pray for the children you know and the people who care for them?

Lord, you gave your Son into the care of Mary and Joseph; grant your wisdom and strength to all who have the responsibility of parenthood.

TONY HORSFALL

Solomon's prayer for wisdom

'Your servant is here among the people you have chosen, a great people, too numerous to count or number. So give your servant a discerning heart to govern your people and to distinguish between right and wrong. For who is able to govern this great people of yours?'

One of the greatest temptations in prayer is to regard it as a means by which we can get God to do what we want, but scripture reminds us that this selfish approach never works: 'When you ask, you do not receive, because you ask with wrong motives, that you may spend what you get on your pleasures' (James 4:3). Solomon could easily have fallen into this trap, for he had been told by God in a dream, 'Ask for whatever you want me to give you' (1 Kings 3:5). He could have asked for long life or wealth, or even the death of his enemies, but instead he asked for something far more crucial—the ability to govern God's people well.

Solomon was aware, as he took over the kingship from his father David, that he was young and inexperienced, and the task before him was a great one. Out of this sense of dependency he asked God for wisdom and discernment so that he could rule well. This pleased God, who granted his request in great measure.

Anyone in leadership should make this prayer their own. The ability to make good decisions is a key skill for any leader, and we will always function best when we are being guided by God and growing in the discernment he gives. When we lead in humility and dependency upon God, we are more likely to make sound choices, which will produce a good outcome and benefit those we lead.

It is important that we ask God to grant wisdom for all in leadership, especially those in local churches or with wider denominational responsibilities. We must pray too for those who lead our nation and make decisions affecting us all, for they too stand in need of the wisdom that comes from God.

Lord, you are the all-wise God. Grant to those who lead us, whether in church or society, the wisdom that they need in these challenging days.

TONY HORSFALL

Elisha's prayer for his servant

'Oh no, my lord. What shall we do?' the servant asked. 'Don't be afraid,' the prophet answered. 'Those who are with us are more than those who are with them.' And Elisha prayed, 'Open his eyes, Lord, so that he may see.' Then the Lord opened the servant's eyes, and he looked and saw the hills full of horses and chariots of fire all round Elisha.

Elisha found himself besieged in the city of Dothan and surrounded by a strong contingent of soldiers belonging to the king of Aram. The Arameans wanted rid of Elisha because, through his prophetic insight, he continually thwarted their plans against Israel by revealing their movements. Naturally, when his young servant saw the enemy forces, he was afraid. There appeared to be no way of escape.

Elisha, however, is unperturbed, for he knows that God is with him and that angel armies are there to protect him. He prays that the servant's eyes might be opened to this invisible heavenly realm. When this happens, the young man is able to see things in a totally different light and his fear evaporates.

This kind of confidence can be ours as well. The apostle Paul declared, 'If God is for us, who can be against us?' (Romans 8:31). There may well be forces arrayed against us—the devil and demonic powers, political systems, and those who hate God—but none of them is a match for the forces of God. Once we know that we are surrounded by God, we can begin to live securely and at peace.

The key to this is that we too have our eyes opened to the invisible realm. When we see things only from a human perspective, they may look bleak indeed, but when we see with the eyes of faith there is always hope. This is the work of God's Spirit, and, if we ask him, he will change our perspective from that of earth to that of heaven, reminding us that God is in control.

Lord, when I see things only through my own understanding, I am often afraid and anxious. Help me to see my circumstances from your divine perspective, so that I can be at peace.

TONY HORSFALL

David's prayer of gratitude

'But who am I, and who are my people, that we should be able to give as generously as this? Everything comes from you, and we have given you only what comes from your hand... Lord our God, all this abundance that we have provided for building you a temple for your Holy Name comes from your hand, and all of it belongs to you.'

King David's great ambition to build a temple for God was handed over to his son Solomon to bring to pass, but this did not prevent him from making preparations for all that would be needed. David himself gave much of the gold, silver, precious stones and other materials from his own resources and inspired others in Israel to give with a similar open-handed generosity, so that everything was provided for this massive project.

Seeing such an amazing provision caused David to burst into praise and prayer. He was conscious that he and his people could give only because God had first given to them. He was overwhelmed by the sheer generosity of God and his heart was enflamed with gratitude.

I wonder if we see God as the source of all that we have. Do we realise that everything we own actually belongs to God, and that we hold it on trust for him? If so, we too will be full of gratitude for the favour he has shown us. Such gratitude creates humility. It makes us realise that we have not earned God's blessing and we do not deserve it. Like David, we begin to ask, 'Who am I to receive such favour?'

Gratitude and humility together create generosity. We cannot hold selfishly on to that which has been given to us, as if it were ours to keep. We are compelled to share what we have been given, and to give as generously as we can to the work of God. Christian people should be among the most generous of all, because we have received not only material blessings but spiritual ones as well.

Why not meditate on these words of Jesus? 'Freely you have received; freely give' (Matthew 10:8). Prayerfully express your gratitude to God.

TONY HORSFALL

Job's prayer of humble response

Then Job replied to the Lord, 'I know that you can do all things; no plan of yours can be thwarted. You asked, "Who is this that obscures my plans without knowledge?" Surely I spoke of things I did not understand, things too wonderful for me to know... My ears had heard of you but now my eyes have seen you. Therefore I despise myself and repent in dust and ashes.'

The story of Job has always held a fascination for Bible readers, especially those trying to understand the problem of suffering. Job is a good and righteous man who loses everything he has for no apparent reason, and then experiences terrible physical suffering. Why has God allowed this? Four of his friends enter into dialogue with Job, trying to answer this question, and insisting that Job must be suffering because he has sinned in some way. Job, however, maintains his innocence and rejects their explanations.

What Job and his friends do not know, but the reader does, is that God has allowed Satan to test him to prove that it is possible for a human being to love God for God's own sake, not just for the blessing he gives. Throughout the turmoil, Job maintains his faith, but the friends' discussions fail to shed light on why he has suffered so much. Only when they have argued themselves to a standstill does God appear to Job in the midst of a storm.

Confronted by the sheer greatness and majesty of God, Job is humbled and repents of his arrogance in thinking he knows better than God or could ever understand his ways. He realises that he must be content to live with mystery and learn to trust God even though he does not understand. His encounter with the presence of God proves more convincing than any intellectual explanation of the reason for his suffering.

In a culture dominated by a scientific worldview, where every cause has an effect and everything a rational explanation, it is humbling to learn that we must sometimes be comfortable with mystery and not-knowing. Trust in the goodness and wisdom of God is what really counts.

Lord, help me to trust even when I don't understand what is happening.

TONY HORSFALL

A prayer for self-awareness

Search me, God, and know my heart; test me and know my anxious thoughts. See if there is any offensive way in me, and lead me in the way everlasting.

Psalm 139 has been described as the most personal of all the psalms, reflecting a deep, intimate relationship between David and his God. David is aware that nothing about him is hidden from the one who knows and sees everything. He is conscious that there is nowhere he can go to hide from the presence of God. He is known by God for who he really is, without pretence or cover-up.

Such a realisation could be unnerving were it not for the fact that even though God knows us as we are, he loves us just the same. True, we may not always welcome such close attention to our behaviour or such scrutiny of our motivations, but once we accept that we are known and loved as we are, we discover a liberating foundation for our relationship with God. We are freed to be our true selves.

Christian discipleship has at its heart the idea of transformation, of personal change and growth. This is possible only if we are willing to face up to the truth about ourselves. David's prayer here reflects a courageous desire for self-discovery. In effect, he is asking God, 'Show me the truth about myself, so that I can change and grow.'

In my personal experience, and from my observation of the many people I have listened to over the years, I am aware that we are all prone to self-deception. We have many clever strategies for hiding our weaknesses from ourselves and others. It takes real courage to be honest and to open ourselves up to the transforming work of God. What makes such vulnerability possible is the knowledge that God has seen the worst about us and yet loves us none the less.

If you desire to grow as a Christian and become a better person, make time for personal reflection and prayerfully consider your ways. You may even find it helpful to talk things over with a trusted friend, counsellor or spiritual director.

Lord, may I know myself even as I am known by you.

TONY HORSFALL

Prayer for renewal of the nation

A prayer of Habakkuk the prophet. On shigionoth*. Lord, I have heard of your fame; I stand in awe of your deeds, Lord. Repeat them in our day, in our time make them known; in wrath remember mercy.*

Habakkuk was a prophet in the late seventh century BC who was deeply troubled by the spiritual state of Judah and the threat from the Babylonians, which was increasing with every day. He was passionate about the injustice, violence and chaos all around him and frustrated because God was seemingly indifferent to his cries for help. He struggled to understand how God could use a wicked nation like Babylon to discipline his people, and was not afraid to voice his complaint to God in prayer.

This little prayer shows his great longing for spiritual renewal and provides us with an incentive to seek a similar spiritual rejuvenation in our own nations. Habakkuk was well aware of the great deeds of God in the past. He was familiar with the stories of creation, of the patriarchs and the birth of the nation, of the exodus from Egypt and so on. Such amazing events caused him to marvel, and yet he remained dissatisfied. Why? Because they were in the past, and Habakkuk was concerned for the present. What would God do *now*?

His cry is that God will again step on to the stage of history and demonstrate his power. He pleads that, although God has every right to be angry, he will in fact choose to be merciful and intervene. He longs for a present-day renewal.

Perhaps, as you look at your own country, you long for such revival. Are you tired of seeing God's standards overthrown and his commandments ignored? Are you pained by the injustices you see—the exploitation of the poor, the victimisation of the vulnerable, the blatant disregard of those most in need? Are you saddened by the state of the church and the way it is sidelined in society?

We can make this prayer our own and refuse to accept the spiritual malaise around us. We too can cry to God that he will move again in our day.

Lord, show your power in this generation. Visit us again, we pray.

TONY HORSFALL

The church prays for boldness

When they heard this, they raised their voices together in prayer to God. 'Sovereign Lord,' they said, 'you made the heavens and the earth and the sea, and everything in them… Now, Lord, consider their threats and enable your servants to speak your word with great boldness. Stretch out your hand to heal and perform signs and wonders through the name of your holy servant Jesus.'

We are reminded here that prayer is not simply a personal matter; it has a corporate dimension as well. Peter and John had been arrested and brought before the Sanhedrin, who commanded them not to preach about Jesus any more. It was an embargo that affected not only the apostles but also every believer in Jerusalem, so, on their release, they gathered together with the other believers to ask God for his help.

This insight into the prayer life of the early church is instructive. The believers are careful not simply to jump in with their requests but first to fix their eyes on the one who is in control—the Sovereign Creator who rules over all. This sense of perspective is vital in prayer. We must remember that the one whom we approach has all power and authority.

Second, their request is clear, direct and relevant. In this situation, what they need is boldness, the confidence to keep on speaking about Jesus even when it may get them into trouble. They also ask that God will bear witness to his word by granting miraculous signs. Notice that they do not ask for the persecution will stop, but that they will be courageous enough to stand firm despite the threats.

At a time when the church is often marginalised and believers are ridiculed, it is easy for us to withdraw into our shells and avoid any kind of public proclamation. Indeed, many believers no longer feel confident in sharing their faith or even declaring themselves to be Christians. The fear of ridicule or censure, particularly in the work environment, silences many. Of course we need wisdom and sensitivity about how to share our faith, but, like the first believers, we also need greater boldness.

Lord, grant to us the same boldness you gave to your church in Jerusalem.

TONY HORSFALL

A prayer for resilience and unity

May the God who gives endurance and encouragement give you the same attitude of mind toward each other that Christ Jesus had, so that with one mind and one voice you may glorify the God and Father of our Lord Jesus Christ.

Over the next few days we will be looking at several prayers from the apostle Paul. It is clear from the epistles that he lived a life of prayer and that he prayed regularly and deeply for the churches for which he cared. His prayers give us a good idea of what to pray for ourselves, our fellow believers and the churches to which we belong.

The letter to the Romans is, in some ways, Paul's *magnum opus*, giving his clearest presentation of the theology behind the gospel message, but it is far from an academic treatise. It breathes with passion and conviction and is undergirded by a deep spirituality that bursts on to the surface in his prayerful concern for the church in Rome. This prayer of blessing contains two key elements: a prayer for endurance and a prayer for unity

'Endurance' is a great Bible word describing the ability to keep going when under extreme pressure, and it is a quality that Paul regarded as fundamental to discipleship. Another word for it would be 'resilience', the ability to bounce back after difficulties, to be strong during trial and to recover from injury or hurt. This is more than dogged determination. It is a quality that is given to us by God and produced in us by the Holy Spirit. This is the only way resilience can be maintained.

In a church where Jew and Gentile were welcomed on equal terms, there was always the possibility of misunderstanding and disharmony. The prayer for unity was therefore vital. Only in Jesus are social divisions removed, so that we can become 'all one in Christ' (Galatians 3:28) regardless of race, gender, generation or social standing. As today's society becomes more fragmented, the need for this kind of unity is just as urgent, and this prayer still as relevant.

If you ever wonder what to pray for your church, here is your answer.

Lord, make us strong, and make us one.

TONY HORSFALL

A prayer for wisdom and revelation

I keep asking that the God of our Lord Jesus Christ, the glorious Father, may give you the Spirit of wisdom and revelation, so that you may know him better. I pray that the eyes of your heart may be enlightened in order that you may know the hope to which he has called you, the riches of his glorious inheritance in his holy people, and his incomparably great power for us who believe.

Paul's letter to Ephesus is one of the 'prison epistles', written while he was confined in Rome. His enforced solitude seems to have brought about a time of deep reflection, when his own understanding of the gospel and the nature of the church was expanded and intensified. Certainly this letter contains some of his loftiest theology, and his prayer here is that his fellow believers would be able to grasp for themselves the wonder of what God has done for them through Christ.

Behind this magnificent prayer are the questions 'How can we know Jesus more fully?' and 'How can we grasp all that is ours in him?' Does progress in the Christian life simply require more effort? Is it dependent upon our intellectual cleverness? Is it easier for some than for others?

Paul suggests that spiritual understanding is dependent neither on intellectual ability nor on striving harder to gain understanding. We learn spiritually because the Holy Spirit teaches us and opens our minds to receive and believe the truth of God. This requires us to ask God to give us 'the Spirit of wisdom and revelation' so that we may indeed know Jesus better. This is why we must pray that the 'eyes of our heart' may be enlightened—that God will enable us to grasp his truth at the core of our being, not just with our minds, so that we are changed and transformed.

Jesus also prayed about this need for revelation: 'I praise you Father, Lord of heaven and earth, because you have hidden these things from the wise and learned, and revealed them to little children' (Matthew 11:25). Clearly this is one prayer that we must all pray if we are to make progress.

Lord, I want to know Jesus better. Grant me the revelation that I need.

TONY HORSFALL

A prayer for strength and love

I pray that out of his glorious riches he may strengthen you with power through his Spirit in your inner being, so that Christ may dwell in your hearts through faith. And I pray that you, being rooted and established in love, may have power, together with all the Lord's holy people, to grasp how wide and long and high and deep is the love of Christ, and to know this love that surpasses knowledge – that you may be filled to the measure of all the fullness of God.

Here is an apostolic prayer that is strategic in content and passionate in delivery. It is perhaps the most vital prayer we can offer for ourselves and others. Paul makes two requests, both built around the word 'power'. The first we can summarise as receiving 'power to live', the second as being given 'power to grasp' the greatness of God's love.

Who does not feel the need for strength to meet the challenges of everyday life? All of us feel inadequate at times, given the demands upon us, and are often aware of our need of strength from outside ourselves. This sense of weakness is no bad thing if it makes us more dependent upon God. Christ has come to live in our hearts through his Spirit. It is the Spirit who empowers us to live in a way that glorifies God.

Alongside this, we need to know how deeply we are loved by God. Such is the greatness of God's love that Paul's words are inadequate to describe it, and he finds himself offering a description that is mathematically impossible: no object can be wide, long, high and deep all at the same time! Truly the love of God is so vast that it surpasses human knowledge. Yet, with the help of God's Spirit, we are enabled to begin to grasp something of that vastness, and to know at least in part that we are the objects of such divine love.

Here are two fundamental truths on which a strong Christian life can be built: a daily empowering by the Spirit who lives within us, and a constant realisation that we are God's beloved children.

Lord, empower me today by your Spirit; pour the love of God into my heart.

TONY HORSFALL

A prayer for depth and discernment

And this is my prayer: that your love may abound more and more in knowledge and depth of insight, so that you may be able to discern what is best and may be pure and blameless for the day of Christ, filled with the fruit of righteousness that comes through Jesus Christ—to the glory and praise of God.

Paul had a particularly close relationship with the church at Philippi, and his affection for them is seen throughout this epistle, specifically in the way he prays for them. Here again we find a pattern of prayer with contemporary relevance.

The heart of his prayer is for the gift of discernment. Discernment is the ability to distinguish between right and wrong, true and false, and also between what is good and what is best. All of us face myriad choices every day, and, in a world of growing complexity, the ability to make good decisions is crucial. Morality and ethics are no longer as straightforward as they used to be, and theological issues that once seemed clear-cut are now less sharply defined. It is easy for us to feel confused and bewildered, as if we have lost our bearings.

Interestingly, in Paul's prayer this request for discernment is linked with a desire for an increase in love—not a wishy-washy sentimental love, but a love that is based upon knowledge and depth of insight. It is not enough to have warm feelings of goodwill towards everybody. What we need is the discerning love that comes from God and mixes truth and grace together in equal amounts. Love without truth will make us naïve; truth without love will make us harsh.

We have seen already (see Monday 23 October) that when Solomon was about to take the lead in Israel, he asked God for a 'discerning heart', a heart infused with the mind of God and able to recognise his will. Such discernment comes through prayer but also by meditating on the scriptures and taking time to mull over decisions until we have a sense of God's peace in our hearts (Colossians 3:15).

Lord, help me in my personal decision-making to discern your will, and grant wisdom to all who lead your church in these confusing times.

TONY HORSFALL

Praying for our nation

I urge, then, first of all, that petitions, prayers, intercession and thanksgiving be made for all people—for kings and all those in authority, that we may live peaceful and quiet lives in all godliness and holiness. This is good, and pleases God our Saviour, who wants all people to be saved and to come to a knowledge of the truth.

While these words are more of an exhortation to pray than an actual prayer, the focus of Paul's concern is so clear that his words feel like a verbalised prayer. He urges Timothy, and the church at Ephesus for which he was responsible, to ensure that they prioritise time to pray for those who are in authority.

The early church benefited greatly from the *Pax Romana*, the period of stability during the time of the Roman empire which meant that travel throughout the Mediterranean world was both practical and safe. Paul himself took advantage of it during his missionary journeys, and the gospel spread rapidly as a result. This is why he urges prayer for political stability: it makes possible the growth of the church.

Regardless of any political persuasion we may have (or not have), it is important that we pray for our nations and their leaders. This was brought home to me with great force when Britain voted to leave the European Union and, for a short period, there was great political insecurity. For the first time I saw how vital the church's role was in praying for all politicians. Their policies and decisions affect every citizen and determine to a large extent the well-being of a nation as a whole.

Churches do not operate in a vacuum but in a context that is greatly shaped by government policies. How important it is, therefore, to pray for humble leaders who see their role as serving the people, whose polices are fair and just, and who are led by God in their decision-making, whether they realise it or not. This kind of prayer is not the most glamorous but it is essential just the same.

Lord, it feels as if we have little influence over the way things are, but we believe that prayer makes a difference. Show us how to pray for our nation.

TONY HORSFALL

A closing prayer

Now may the God of peace, who through the blood of the eternal covenant brought back from the dead our Lord Jesus, that great Shepherd of the sheep, equip you with everything good for doing his will, and may he work in us what is pleasing to him, through Jesus Christ, to whom be glory for ever and ever.

I first came across this prayer when it was used as a doxology at the close of a service I attended, and it seems appropriate to use it as the final prayer in these readings. With its themes of equipping and empowering, it prepares us for the work of serving Christ in our daily lives.

In this prayer we are reminded who God is (the God of peace) and that our relationship with him is based securely upon the new covenant; also that Jesus not only died but is risen and continues to care for us as the Shepherd of the sheep. These are inspiring thoughts to bring into any prayer and are the foundation for two strategic requests.

The first request is that we may be equipped with everything we need to do God's will. We are not expected to busy ourselves with the work of God's kingdom using simply natural abilities. There are gifts that God wants to give us so that we can serve effectively. Each of us is given some gift by which we can make our own unique contribution—for example, serving, teaching, encouraging, giving, leading or caring (Romans 12:7–8). Part of our maturing as disciples comes as we identify our gifts, perhaps with the help of other people, and then use them to serve God.

The second request is for God to be at work in us, enabling us to serve in a way that brings glory to Jesus. Not only does God give us gifts to use, but he enables and empowers us to operate those same gifts. God works in us through the Holy Spirit, motivating us to serve and giving us the strength to do so. None of us could sustain our service without this divine enabling.

Risen Lord Jesus, equip us with all we need to serve you,
and work in us the desire to please you.

TONY HORSFALL

From suffering to hope: Psalms 73—80

What happens to your faith when your life goes wrong? Does it grow weaker or stronger? Do you turn to others, perhaps in your church, for help and encouragement, or do you say, 'I can handle this alone'? Or do you belong to a church where suffering is seen as evidence of personal sin? Most importantly, do you assume that God is no longer there or interested, or do you turn to God even more, asking for wisdom, clarity and guidance?

Old Testament scholar Walter Brueggemann describes many of the psalms as having a common movement: from 'orientation' (knowing where you are, where you 'stand'), through 'disorientation' (being confused and thrown off course by circumstance), to 'reorientation' (finding a new, deeper way to see the world and God). I certainly see that pattern in these psalms from the middle of the book. Many of them stem from a time when the promised land, after its division into two kingdoms, was under attack or invaded by its more powerful neighbours—either Israel by Assyria in the eighth century or Judah by Babylon in the sixth. Understandably, the people were asking whether God was still on their side, whether they were still 'chosen'.

Other psalms were clearly triggered by the individual writer's suffering. Many of this selection are headed as written by Asaph rather than the more well-known David, who would become Israel's most famous king. Whether communal or individual, they nearly all contain a sense that it has become harder to understand what is happening and what God is up to. Many end with a sense that, after being honest with God about their feelings, the psalmist and his people have come to a deeper sense that God is in charge. Open lament leads to reconnection with God, new hope and new purpose.

How can we use these psalms in our daily or weekly worship? Not by omitting the despairing bits and only sharing the 'everything's all right now' parts, which is what we too often do. I've made some suggestions in my comments, and I am sure you can think of more. The psalms are always a great way of using scripture to be honest with God and each other.

VERONICA ZUNDEL

How the other half lives

Truly God is good to the upright, to those who are pure in heart. But as for me, my feet had almost stumbled; my steps had nearly slipped. For I was envious of the arrogant; I saw the prosperity of the wicked. For they have no pain; their bodies are sound and sleek. They are not in trouble as others are; they are not plagued like other people. Therefore pride is their necklace; violence covers them like a garment... Therefore the people turn and praise them, and find no fault in them.

Last year I did a course in the Enneagram, a personality-type tool. Each of the nine types has its 'shadow side', its besetting sin. When I found out that the shadow of Type Four, the Romantic, was envy, I knew for sure that that was my type!

If your life is hard and you see others apparently having no troubles, it is easy to feel there is no justice. Nationally and internationally, it is not the caring, the faithful or the generous who get all the privileges and acclaim; often it is the shallow, the corrupt and those who know how to play the system—or, indeed, those who were just born healthy and wealthy.

What are we to think? We will look at the psalmist's answer tomorrow, but for now consider this: envy brings us no happiness, it just adds to our unhappiness. Rather than trying to make our lives like someone else's, it is better to use what we have to work for others' welfare, to fight injustice, to raise those who are 'on the bottom of the heap'.

Ultimately, we cannot know why those who have done nothing to merit it have easy lives, while our own seem to be full of disasters. But the Beatitudes suggest that in God's eyes, it is the weak, the troubled and the marginalised who are at the heart of God's purposes: 'Blessed are the poor in spirit, for theirs is the kingdom of heaven. Blessed are those who mourn, for they will be comforted' (Matthew 5:3–4).

'All in vain I have kept my heart clean and washed my hands in innocence'
(Psalm 73:13). If this is how you feel, talk to God about it.

VERONICA ZUNDEL

Seeing the big picture

If I had said, 'I will talk on in this way', I would have been untrue to the circle of your children. But when I thought how to understand this, it seemed to me a wearisome task, until I went into the sanctuary of God; then I perceived their end. Truly you set them in slippery places; you make them fall to ruin. How they are destroyed in a moment, swept away utterly by terrors! They are like a dream when one awakes; on awaking you despise their phantoms.

As a child, after one of my frequent rows with my mother (I can't remember what a single one was about!), I would storm out of the house and go to the nearby railway halt, where I would stand on the footbridge and look down over the tracks. Somehow, taking 'the long view' put everything in perspective.

The psalmist takes the long view here, historically rather than geographically. There is a great reversal coming. Mary prophesied it first: 'He has brought down the powerful from their thrones, and lifted up the lowly; he has filled the hungry with good things, and sent the rich away empty' (Luke 1:52–53). Then Jesus affirmed it: 'But many who are first will be last, and the last will be first' (Mark 10:31). Although we live in a world of injustice, where good things happen to bad people and vice versa, there will be justice at last, and God's justice is way beyond our own inadequate efforts.

Even in this life, the powerful sometimes fall from grace, and the nobodies are sometimes lifted to the heights. But we are not to gloat over celebrities who fall off their pedestals; we may rejoice in the defeat of evil but not in the shaming of people.

If he had continued in his envy, the psalmist declares, 'I would have been untrue to the circle of your children.' It is our fellow believers' job to recall us to the 'God's-eye view' of the world, and ours to do the same for them.

'Whom have I in heaven but you? And there is nothing on earth that I desire other than you' (Psalm 73:25). Make this your prayer.

VERONICA ZUNDEL

Remember your people

O God, why do you cast us off for ever? Why does your anger smoke against the sheep of your pasture? Remember your congregation, which you acquired long ago, which you redeemed to be the tribe of your heritage. Remember Mount Zion, where you came to dwell... Your foes have roared within your holy place; they set up their emblems there. At the upper entrance they hacked the wooden trellis with axes. And then, with hatchets and hammers, they smashed all its carved work. They set your sanctuary on fire; they desecrated the dwelling-place of your name, bringing it to the ground. They said to themselves, 'We will utterly subdue them'; they burned all the meeting-places of God in the land.

A friend of a friend collects architectural features from demolished buildings—a stair newel, a door knob, a piece of plaster moulding. It is always sad when a beloved place is lost or damaged. So I find the details here of the destruction wrought by Israel's enemies very poignant—and more so because the place was holy, the focus of the people's meetings with God.

We have moved, in this psalm, from personal woes to communal tragedy. Early in 2016, my church closed down. We did not have our own building, but the people, through whom I met with God every week, are dispersed and feeling spiritually orphaned. The psalmist too, in the face of destruction, asks God to remember not so much the precious wood carvings (though he is sad about those) but 'your congregation'. It is the people who are the dwelling place of God; the building is just a practical necessity, its beauty a tribute to the beauty of the God it honours.

Many people, when facing disaster, conclude that either there is no God or that God is against them, that they must have done something wrong. The psalmist takes a different path: he cries out to God to take notice. His arguments are both emotional and rational. Why would God choose a particular people and then reject them?

Tomorrow we will see how God answers.

What questions do you want to ask God about your own experience or that of a group to which you belong?

VERONICA ZUNDEL

Reminding God

Yet God my King is from of old, working salvation in the earth. You divided the sea by your might; you broke the heads of the dragons in the waters. You crushed the heads of Leviathan; you gave him as food for the creatures of the wilderness. You cut openings for springs and torrents; you dried up ever-flowing streams. Yours is the day, yours also the night; you established the luminaries and the sun. You have fixed all the bounds of the earth; you made summer and winter... Have regard for your covenant, for the dark places of the land are full of the haunts of violence. Do not let the downtrodden be put to shame; let the poor and needy praise your name... Do not forget the clamour of your foes, the uproar of your adversaries that goes up continually.

Research shows that time spent in nature is good for children with conditions such as Attention Deficit Disorder. There is something restorative about immersing ourselves in the natural world. Like Job, the psalmist turns to creation for a reminder of God's power to overcome what threatens us. God can vanquish the 'monsters' in our lives, as well as provide for our hunger and thirst, whether physical or spiritual.

The writer also reminds God of two things: that God has made a covenant with God's people, and that the 'name', the reputation, of God is at stake when there is injustice or inequality in this world. We help the poor and needy not just because they need it but because God wants us to take part in creating a world where there are no poor and needy. Only such a world is worthy of its maker.

Finally, the psalmist reminds God not to forget how oppressed and downcast God's people are in the face of their enemies. Does God really need reminding? No, but the psalmist needs to remind God, to feel that his cry for help has been heard. Our prayers do not necessarily change God's mind, but they reveal God's mind to us.

'The dark places of the land are full of the haunts of violence' (v. 20b);
'Yours is the day, yours also the night' (v. 16). How do these statements
balance each other?

VERONICA ZUNDEL

God has not forgotten

We give thanks to you, O God; we give thanks; your name is near. People tell of your wondrous deeds. At the set time that I appoint I will judge with equity. When the earth totters, with all its inhabitants, it is I who keep its pillars steady. I say to the boastful, 'Do not boast', and to the wicked, 'Do not lift up your horn; do not lift up your horn on high, or speak with insolent neck'.... For in the hand of the Lord there is a cup with foaming wine, well mixed; he will pour a draught from it, and all the wicked of the earth shall drain it down to the dregs. But I will rejoice for ever; I will sing praises to the God of Jacob.

Language is full of images and pictures, but the images of one culture are not always obvious to another. For example, the biblical image of people as sheep will not make sense in a country that has no sheep. So what's all this about horns and cups?

The horn, in biblical terms, stands for pride and power, of nations as well as individuals. 'Insolent neck' we can probably all understand: we still sometimes use the phrase 'brass neck' to mean brazen insolence. The cup, in the prophetic writings, represents not a welcome drink but something more like an unpleasant medicine or even poison—that is, the punishment awaiting evildoers. And while the writers of the psalms probably didn't believe that the earth had literal pillars, they are a strong image of stability and firmness.

This short psalm, then, affirms God's plan to bring true justice to the earth. Justice may seem a long way away, especially when television reports major on bad news and catastrophe (there is good news, but it is rarely reported). However, 'your name is near' (v. 1); the great Day of the Lord may still be far away, but God is not. Thus we can praise God for the redemption that hasn't happened yet. It has, after all, already begun in Jesus, and in our lives if we belong to him.

'All the horns of the wicked I will cut off, but the horns of the righteous shall be exalted' (Psalm 75:10).

VERONICA ZUNDEL

An angry God?

In Judah God is known, his name is great in Israel. His abode has been established in Salem, his dwelling-place in Zion. There he broke the flashing arrows, the shield, the sword, and the weapons of war. Glorious are you, more majestic than the everlasting mountains. The stout-hearted were stripped of their spoil; they sank into sleep; none of the troops was able to lift a hand. At your rebuke, O God of Jacob, both rider and horse lay stunned. But you indeed are awesome! Who can stand before you when once your anger is roused?... Make vows to the Lord your God, and perform them; let all who are around him bring gifts to the one who is awesome, who cuts off the spirit of princes, who inspires fear in the kings of the earth.

'The wrath of God' is a concept many of us struggle with. How do we reconcile it with the love of God? And is the cross really about Jesus holding back God's anger from us?

I sometimes think of God's anger as something like that of a mother who has found her child after losing her or him in a crowded place. She may burst out in apparent fury, 'Where on earth have you been?' but her anger is just an expression of her wounded love, a relief from the fear she felt. This is an emotional, involved anger rather than a cold, distant one; and this is how the Bible, which has no problem with ascribing emotions to God, portrays it.

We can also remember that God's anger is primarily directed not at people but at oppression, exploitation, and all the destructive things that people do. The psalmist's triumph is not at the fact that Israel's enemies have been killed, but at the fact that the danger they represented has been lifted.

As for the cross, there are many ways to understand it. What makes most sense to me is the idea that, by participating in our suffering and death, God defeats suffering and death. Punishment of sins is an element of God's work, but not the only aspect. Love always trumps it.

'In Christ God was reconciling the world to himself, not counting their trespasses against them' (2 Corinthians 5:19).

VERONICA ZUNDEL

When God 'turns away'

I cry aloud to God, aloud to God, that he may hear me. In the day of my trouble I seek the Lord; in the night my hand is stretched out without wearying; my soul refuses to be comforted. I think of God, and I moan; I meditate, and my spirit faints. You keep my eyelids from closing; I am so troubled that I cannot speak. I consider the days of old, and remember the years of long ago... 'Will the Lord spurn for ever, and never again be favourable? Has his steadfast love ceased for ever? Are his promises at an end for all time? Has God forgotten to be gracious? Has he in anger shut up his compassion?' And I say, 'It is my grief that the right hand of the Most High has changed.'

Does God ever give up on us? It can feel that way when our lives fall apart and we simply can't cope. Sleep may elude us, and distress may mean we cannot even get the words out to say how bad we feel. In Jewish custom, after a bereavement, friends will take turns to sit in silence with the bereaved person or family for seven days after the death. We Christians might also do well to keep our mouths shut when facing someone else's sorrow. Too often we rush in with simplistic solutions.

But note: the writer has not lost his 'inner voice', the one that cries out to God, day and night, to bring him out of his troubles. He meditates on God's nature, on how God has blessed him or others in the past, perhaps on how he has come through previous times of trouble. His cries are not just petitions for help, but hard questions. Has God stopped loving him? Have God's promises ceased to apply? Has anger overcome God's compassion? He even voices his worst fear—that God has turned the face of divine love away from him.

This honesty is itself therapeutic, even before answers come.

Job's three friends 'sat with him on the ground for seven days and seven nights, and no one spoke a word to him, for they saw that his suffering was very great' (Job 2:13).

VERONICA ZUNDEL

Shifting the telescope

I will call to mind the deeds of the Lord; I will remember your wonders of old. I will meditate on all your work, and muse on your mighty deeds... When the waters saw you, O God, when the waters saw you, they were afraid; the very deep trembled. The clouds poured out water; the skies thundered; your arrows flashed on every side. The crash of your thunder was in the whirlwind; your lightnings lit up the world; the earth trembled and shook. Your way was through the sea, your path, through the mighty waters; yet your footprints were unseen. You led your people like a flock by the hand of Moses and Aaron.

Last weekend my family and I went up the Shard skyscraper in London to see the view (which we just caught before mist descended and hid it all). As well as the spectacular sights out of the windows, there were digital telescopes with screens, which could zoom in on particular locations. If you rotated the telescope a bit, you would get a totally different picture. You could also view historic panoramas of the city, or the city at night or in different weather—images of the past which illuminated the present.

In Cognitive Behaviour Therapy, an approach that has helped me with chronic depression, the aim is to identify negative thoughts and behaviours and replace them with positive ones. I think the psalmist is practising a kind of 'spiritual behaviour therapy', or what psychologists call 'reframing', here. From dwelling on his sorrows, he resolves to focus on God and the blessings God has given him and his people. This is not a teeth-gritting fight to ignore the negative; rather, it is 'realigning the telescope', training it on to sunnier times and a more positive view. The God he finds is a determined, dynamic God, not sitting on a throne on high but swooping like a parent to grab his endangered children and pluck them out of slavery. As in Psalm 29, the storm is a vivid image of God's power— yet 'your footprints were unseen'.

'Set your minds on things that are above, not on things that are on earth'
(Colossians 3:2). What we see depends on where we look.

VERONICA ZUNDEL

Teach your children well

Give ear, O my people, to my teaching; incline your ears to the words of my mouth. I will open my mouth in a parable; I will utter dark sayings from of old, things that we have heard and known, that our ancestors have told us. We will not hide them from their children; we will tell to the coming generation the glorious deeds of the Lord, and his might, and the wonders that he has done. He established a decree in Jacob, and appointed a law in Israel, which he commanded our ancestors to teach to their children; that the next generation might know them, the children yet unborn, and rise up and tell them to their children, so that they should set their hope in God, and not forget the works of God, but keep his commandments; and that they should not be like their ancestors, a stubborn and rebellious generation... whose spirit was not faithful to God.

Recently I've been trying to write a memoir of my family and especially my late brother. I'm helped by a two-hour film of my mother telling her early life story for the Shoah Foundation, which records the memories of Holocaust survivors and refugees. As I write, all the family stories and sayings come flooding back—some funny, some poignant.

In many Holocaust families, the parents told their children nothing about their past, or refused to speak their native language. One friend didn't even know she was Jewish till she went through her mother's papers. Perhaps it was all too painful. My family wasn't like that: we spoke a mixture of English and German, and stories of the past (though not the most difficult) were daily currency.

This is the longest psalm in our selection for this fortnight, and it follows on naturally from yesterday's, filling in the content of what the psalmist might have been meditating on as he sought a way out of anguish. Essentially, it's about keeping the family memories alive, only the family in question is the whole of God's people, and the main actor is not the people themselves but God.

Is it hard to tell your children, or others' children, about what God has done for you? If so, ask God for help.

VERONICA ZUNDEL

Truthful memories

In the sight of their ancestors he worked marvels in the land of Egypt...
He divided the sea and let them pass through it, and made the waters
stand like a heap. In the daytime he led them with a cloud, and all night
long with a fiery light. He split rocks open in the wilderness, and gave
them drink abundantly as from the deep. ..Yet they sinned still more
against him, rebelling against the Most High in the desert. They tested
God in their heart by demanding the food they craved. They spoke
against God, saying, 'Can God spread a table in the wilderness? Even
though he struck the rock so that water gushed out and torrents
overflowed, can he also give bread, or provide meat for his people?'

Although my Mennonite church stopped meeting for Sunday worship in
March 2016, we have maintained our online archive of sermons preached
by our various regular and guest preachers (we were a lay-led congregation). The 'Preaching Peace' blog starts with a sermon preached when we
knew our church life was coming to an end. It states, 'These sermons are
our congregation's testament to a church life well lived. "We are pilgrims
on a journey," we sang together frequently. Like pilgrims, we leave traces
of our journey behind.'

We can see the same process in this psalm, which recollects the key
moments of the Israelites' journey from slavery in Egypt to freedom in the
promised land. However, it also records their frequent doubt and disobedience. (I hope our Mennonite sermons are honest about our weaknesses
too!) Even when God has freed, led and provided, the people are still
sceptical about his ability, or willingness, to continue providing. Scholars
have observed that this is how we know the truthfulness of the Bible—
because its authors do not portray flawless spiritual heroes but are honest about the broken humanity of its characters.

Of course the psalmist is writing about the sins of his ancestors, not his
own; this is always easier! To admit to one's own failings is harder.

*'Write the vision; make it plain on tablets, so that a runner may read it'
(Habakkuk 2:2). What memories of your own or your church's life might
you need to record?*

VERONICA ZUNDEL

Enemy love

They did not keep in mind his power, or the day when he redeemed them from the foe; when he displayed his signs in Egypt... He turned their rivers to blood, so that they could not drink of their streams. He sent among them swarms of flies, which devoured them, and frogs, which destroyed them. He gave their crops to the caterpillar, and the fruit of their labour to the locust. He destroyed their vines with hail, and their sycamores with frost. He gave over their cattle to the hail, and their flocks to thunderbolts... He struck all the firstborn in Egypt... Then he led out his people like sheep, and guided them in the wilderness like a flock... He drove out nations before them; he apportioned them for a possession and settled the tribes of Israel in their tents.

One practice of my church was to hold a (somewhat Christianised) Passover meal each year. This included a ritual in which we recited the ten plagues of Egypt, dipping our finger in wine for each plague, and dropping the wine on to our plates, to commemorate the Egyptian blood that was shed.

Where there are winners, there must also be losers. The Jewish people developed this custom to show regret that, to free the Jews, and because of Pharaoh's obstinacy, God had to punish the people of Egypt. Their instincts were right: we should not withhold compassion from our enemies, for God does not. God never stopped loving each Egyptian, and we cannot predict their ultimate fate in God's hands.

It is human nature to enjoy the destruction of forces seen by us as evil, but it is nothing to be proud of. The psalmist does not rejoice over Egyptian suffering or over the nations that were driven out for the chosen people. Instead he sees them as signs of how determined God was to create a nation who would show the rest of the world how to honour God and how to practise justice, peace and compassion. When they fail to do this, as the psalmist warns by recalling their history, then they lose their entitlement to the land.

'While we were enemies, we were reconciled to God through the death of his Son' (Romans 5:10). How can we love enemies?

VERONICA ZUNDEL

War is hell

O God, the nations have come into your inheritance; they have defiled your holy temple; they have laid Jerusalem in ruins. They have given the bodies of your servants to the birds of the air for food, the flesh of your faithful to the wild animals of the earth. They have poured out their blood like water all around Jerusalem, and there was no one to bury them. We have become a taunt to our neighbors, mocked and derided by those around us. How long, O Lord? Will you be angry for ever? Will your jealous wrath burn like fire? Pour out your anger on the nations that do not know you, and on the kingdoms that do not call on your name. For they have devoured Jacob and laid waste his habitation.

When you read this, I pray that the war in Syria, longer now than World War II, will be over. As I write, a fragile ceasefire has just been started, but we cannot know if it will hold. War is always terrible. Modern weapons kill indiscriminately, and soldiers return traumatised by what they have seen. We have all seen the pictures on television of mass graves and flattened cities.

It has always been the same; the only difference now is that we have more powerful weaponry. Here the psalmist laments, in great detail, the death, destruction and even sacrilege that the invading troops have brought. There are too many dead even to keep up with burying them, so the bodies are left for the vultures and jackals.

How do we, most of whom live in safety and security, pray for those who have to live day by day in the midst of war and terror, who have no shelter, food or water? We could start by trying to hear their voices in our worship—perhaps by reading quotes from a news report before intercessions, or getting prayer resources from Christian Aid.

And what do we do with the psalmist's desire for God to 'pour anger' on the aggressor? At least it is honest, and he leaves it to God rather than taking revenge himself.

The psalmist's prayer in the midst of suffering is a passionate one.
Our prayers, too, should be passionate—even if we're British!

VERONICA ZUNDEL

God in the spotlight

Do not remember against us the iniquities of our ancestors; let your compassion come speedily to meet us, for we are brought very low. Help us, O God of our salvation, for the glory of your name; deliver us, and forgive our sins, for your name's sake. Why should the nations say, 'Where is their God?' Let the avenging of the outpoured blood of your servants be known among the nations before our eyes. Let the groans of the prisoners come before you; according to your great power preserve those doomed to die. Return sevenfold into the bosom of our neighbours the taunts with which they taunted you, O Lord! Then we your people, the flock of your pasture, will give thanks to you for ever; from generation to generation we will recount your praise.

Have you ever been unjustly accused of something? If so, you will know the feeling of wanting to clear your name. For the people of the Bible, however, their chief concern was for God's reputation. That depended on how God's people were doing, for when their land was invaded or attacked, when their harvest failed or they simply weren't flourishing, it reflected badly on their belief in the one true God. Other nations could claim that their 'gods' were stronger and more generous.

We still sometimes think this way today. If our lives are always difficult, we think we are not a good witness to our faith. But in reality, being a Christian is not about everything always going well. It's about how we respond to what happens to us—with hopelessness and despair, or with trust in God.

It is not our sufferings that are 'a bad witness' to the world. It is when we quarrel, when we lack compassion, when we demonise people who are different from us, or when we fail to practise 'good disagreement', that people may justifiably ask, 'Where is their God?'

'We are afflicted in every way, but not crushed; perplexed, but not driven to despair; persecuted, but not forsaken; struck down, but not destroyed; always carrying in the body the death of Jesus, so that the life of Jesus may also be made visible in our bodies' (2 Corinthians 4:8–10).

VERONICA ZUNDEL

The vine

Give ear, O Shepherd of Israel, you who lead Joseph like a flock! You who are enthroned upon the cherubim, shine forth… Stir up your might, and come to save us!… You brought a vine out of Egypt; you drove out the nations and planted it. You cleared the ground for it; it took deep root and filled the land. The mountains were covered with its shade, the mighty cedars with its branches; it sent out its branches to the sea, and its shoots to the River. Why then have you broken down its walls, so that all who pass along the way pluck its fruit? The boar from the forest ravages it, and all that move in the field feed on it. Turn again, O God of hosts; look down from heaven, and see; have regard for this vine, the stock that your right hand planted… Then we will never turn back from you; give us life, and we will call on your name.

I'm not a gardener, but I love to visit other people's creative, cared-for gardens when they're open for the National Gardens Scheme, or to sit in a retreat house garden in the sun or shade.

This image of God's people as a vine, giving shade and fruit to all, is a common one in the Old Testament, especially in the prophets. Jesus reapplies it to himself as the fulfilment of their witness: 'I am the true vine, and my Father is the vine-grower… Abide in me as I abide in you' (John 15:1, 4). We, his disciples, can reapply it to ourselves as we gather and grow into a people giving shelter and blessing to the world. Do our churches give this kind of welcome?

For the psalmist, the sheltering wall that protected the vine is broken down, and the fruit is given to those who will neither appreciate nor share it. Perhaps your church life feels this way at the moment, because of conflict or opposition. I certainly feel that way about the closure of my beloved church. But remember, 'Every branch that bears fruit he prunes to make it bear more fruit' (John 15:2).

---

*'Restore us, O Lord God of hosts; let your face shine, that we may be saved'
(Psalm 80:19).*

VERONICA ZUNDEL

Wilderness

The words 'wilderness' and 'desert' are used interchangeably in the Bible, occurring 245 times in the Old Testament and 35 times in the New. A diverse range of geographical locations is described, from largely uninhabited but reasonably well-watered grazing land, surrounding villages and towns, to the most arid and desolate places. However, the biblical emphasis is usually on what happens to those in the wilderness, rather than focusing on the location. Wilderness is where the challenges presented by the environment bring issues of faith into focus.

If wilderness describes the physical manifestation of arid and life-threatening conditions, it also came to be used as a description of the emotions experienced by someone whose faith was under pressure. Many biblical stories, from the valley of dry bones in Ezekiel to Elijah's flight in 1 Kings, use the physical location to paint a spiritual portrait. We continue to describe times of spiritual challenge and aridity as our own 'wilderness experiences'. But if wilderness might feel like, and certainly could be, a place of judgement, it was also a place of revelation, renewal and safety. In the first week of these readings we will look at the importance of wilderness as a place of experiencing God.

One of the dominant themes of the Old and New Testaments is the story of the exodus, in which God deliberately led his people into the wilderness as they fled from Egypt. The extreme environment evoked reactions from the people that often turned into outright hostility, yet it was in this environment that God demonstrated his faithfulness and love by guiding, protecting and nourishing them. This journey in the wilderness became understood as the formative experience of Israel's journey of faith.

But wilderness was not confined to that single event. The importance of experiencing God in wilderness is a recurring theme in the scriptures. Isaiah speaks of the restoration after the exile in Babylon as a new journey through the wilderness; Jesus must first overcome his temptations in the wilderness before embarking on his ministry; Paul writing to the Corinthians, and John in the book of Revelation, both refer to the wilderness experiences of their contemporary churches. In the second week of notes, we will look at how wilderness might contribute to our own faith development.

NICK READ

Wilderness: a place of judgement

I will bring you from the nations and gather you from the countries where you have been scattered—with a mighty hand and an out-stretched arm and with outpoured wrath. I will bring you into the wilderness of the nations and there, face to face, I will execute judgement upon you. As I judged your ancestors in the wilderness of the land of Egypt, so I will judge you, declares the Sovereign Lord. I will take note of you as you pass under my rod, and I will bring you into the bond of the covenant.

The cataclysmic event in Judah's history was the fall of Jerusalem in 586BC and the dispersion of the people, including those exiled to Babylon. After many years in exile came the restoration and the return to their homeland. But it begged the question: who or what was to be restored? After decades of living among people of different faiths and traditions, what was left that was authentic about being the people of God?

To answer that question, God needed to execute a judgement. The parallel is drawn very clearly: just as God judged their forefathers in the wilderness during the exodus, so a similar event is envisaged in which God brings this new generation into the 'wilderness of the nations'. It is in the wilderness that God is 'face to face' with his people; there is nowhere to hide and no distraction. While at first sight that is totally discomfiting, the promise that was given to those who remained faithful was of restoration: they would be restored to the bond of the covenant. The fulfilment of the promise is recorded in the renewal of the covenant in Nehemiah 9:38.

At times we will also need to be brought back to God from the alternative paths that we have embraced. We come under judgement, when our thoughts and actions are sifted and found wanting. The desert is an appropriate description of where we may find ourselves, but God has no intention of leaving us there indefinitely.

'Though he brings grief, he will show compassion,
so great is his unfailing love' (Lamentations 3:32).

NICK READ

Wilderness: a place of revelation

On the first day of the third month after the Israelites left Egypt—on that very day—they came to the Desert of Sinai. After they set out from Rephidim, they entered the Desert of Sinai, and Israel camped there in the desert in front of the mountain. Then Moses went up to God, and the Lord called to him from the mountain and said, 'This is what you are to say to the descendants of Jacob and what you are to tell the people of Israel: "You yourselves have seen what I did to Egypt, and how I carried you on eagles' wings and brought you to myself. Now if you obey me fully and keep my covenant, then out of all nations you will be my treasured possession. Although the whole earth is mine, you will be for me a kingdom of priests and a holy nation."'

This reading from Exodus 19 is the start of the narrative of the ten commandments, the giving of the law, and it is no accident that it occurs in 'the Desert'. The people are at neither the beginning nor the end of their journey. Jacob also received his two great revelations, the vision of a ladder stretching from earth to heaven (Genesis 28:10–17) and the wrestling match with a stranger (32:22–32) in the midst of journeys, in places that were 'in between'. Although the history of Israel may centre on the promised land, it is punctuated throughout by wilderness experiences and exile, and in every case these are places of revelation.

The giving of the law within the desert transcends place. Had the Israelites received the law after they had entered the promised land, it would for ever have been associated with that land. Any subsequent exile would have marked the end of the covenant. But the God of Israel is not to be tied to a particular place or time. He is the God of the desert, who defies all attempts to tie him down; he can be found everywhere and worshipped everywhere.

---

*'I remember the devotion of your youth, how as a bride you loved me
and followed me through the wilderness, through a land not sown'
(Jeremiah 2:2).*

NICK READ

Wilderness: a place of renewal

The hand of the Lord was on me, and he brought me out by the Spirit of the Lord and set me in the middle of a valley; it was full of bones. He led me to and fro among them, and I saw a great many bones on the floor of the valley, bones that were very dry. He asked me, 'Son of man, can these bones live?' I said, 'Sovereign Lord, you alone know.' Then he said to me, 'Prophesy to these bones and say to them, "Dry bones, hear the word of the Lord!"'

Perhaps the starkest evocation of wilderness within the scriptures is the valley of dry bones, a totally arid and lifeless location. We know from the text that this is a metaphor for the house of Israel (Ezekiel 37:11), but it is not just an expression of spiritual barrenness; it is a reflection of their physical reality. Israel was in a foreign land, in exile, depressed and helpless. It's a stark metaphor: the bones are 'very dry' implying that they have been bleached in the sun for many years.

Someone was needed to bring them an authentic word of God's power and restore them to hope. It was Ezekiel who was entrusted with the task, but he had no answers or solutions within himself. Only the Sovereign Lord knew whether these bones could be brought back to life. Nevertheless, the word of the Lord that was delivered to the nation through Ezekiel was, 'I will put my Spirit in you and you will live, and I will settle you in your own land' (37:14). The revival of the dry bones signified God's plan for the nation's future restoration. Most importantly, though, it showed that their new life was dependent not on the circumstances of their current predicament but on God's sovereign power.

'But because of his great love for us, God, who is rich in mercy, made us alive with Christ even when we were dead in transgressions—it is by grace you have been saved. And God raised us up with Christ and seated us with him in the heavenly realms in Christ Jesus' (Ephesians 2:4–6).

NICK READ

Wilderness: a place of safety

When the dragon saw that he had been hurled to the earth, he pursued the woman who had given birth to the male child. The woman was given the two wings of a great eagle, so that she might fly to the place prepared for her in the wilderness, where she would be taken care of for a time, times and half a time, out of the snake's reach.

The most dramatic account of the wilderness as a place of refuge is found in the book of Revelation. The book is rich in Old Testament imagery and needs careful unpacking. This passage tells of a spiritual battle taking place on earth. The dragon, representing forces opposed to God, has been expelled from heaven and hurled to the earth, where his relentless opposition continues against 'the woman who had given birth to the male child', a metaphor for Israel as the mother of the Messiah, and of the new Israel, the church.

The church's response to this threat is a version of the exodus story. As God brought his people on eagles' wings into the wilderness (Exodus 19:4), where they were nourished for 42 years, so in John's vision the church is also 'given the two wings of a great eagle' to fly 'to the place prepared for her in the wilderness'. The role of the desert continues, where it is understood both as a place of refuge for God's people (for example, Hagar in Genesis 16:1-13; Moses in Exodus 2:15—3:1; and David in 1 Samuel 23:25), and as the place of preparation before the people can enter into the promised land.

It is John's assertion that the desert experience will be a continuing facet of the church's life. The passage is significant in that while it offers assurance of divine care, it does not offer exemption from suffering. The church will assuredly be led by God, and the church will be protected by God, but the wilderness nevertheless remains a place of danger and desolation.

Give thanks for the times and places when you have found sanctuary in your Christian life.

NICK READ

Wilderness: a school for faith

A voice of one calling: 'In the wilderness prepare the way for the Lord; make straight in the desert a highway for our God. Every valley shall be raised up, every mountain and hill made low; the rough ground shall become level, the rugged places a plain. And the glory of the Lord will be revealed, and all people will see it together. For the mouth of the Lord has spoken.'

In Isaiah's prophetic words, the revelation of God starts in the desert, it is in the wilderness that the way of God is to be prepared, and it is the wilderness that is to be transformed by God's presence. The exodus and the 40 years in the wilderness after the escape from Egypt was a formative time in the history of Israel, but it was not unique. In Isaiah's prophecy, a new exodus is envisaged as the people return from exile in Babylon to their home. Wilderness will, once again, become the focus of God's activity. It suggests that wilderness is not a once-in-a-lifetime phenomenon, but part of the cycle of God's dealings with his people and an essential constituent of God's continuing revelation. The prophet Hosea echoes similar sentiments, in which Israel is to be led into the desert to allow God to speak with her (Hosea 2:14–15).

In the New Testament, John the Baptist would be understood as the fulfilment of Isaiah's prophecy, the voice in the wilderness who would herald the fullest revelation of God in Jesus; but again it starts in the desert. Wilderness, therefore, when experienced by individuals, is not to be understood as a sign of failure or of judgement but as the precursor to deeper revelation. We should note, however, that Isaiah does not underestimate the difficulties of maintaining that perspective in the reality of a wilderness experience in which 'all people are like grass' (40:6).

'It is a commonplace of all religious thought, even the most primitive, that the man seeking visions and insight must go apart from his fellows and love for a time in the wilderness' (Loren Eiseley, American anthropologist and philosopher).

NICK READ

Elijah in the wilderness

Elijah was afraid and ran for his life. When he came to Beersheba in Judah, he left his servant there, while he himself went a day's journey into the wilderness. He came to a broom bush, sat down under it and prayed that he might die. 'I have had enough, Lord,' he said. 'Take my life; I am no better than my ancestors.' Then he lay down under the bush and fell asleep.

Elijah's despair was real. He was fleeing for his life from a vengeful Jezebel and headed for the safety of the desert. After a tiring journey, he sat under the shade of a broom tree and begged to be allowed to die, such was his emotional state. Exhausted, he fell asleep. In this story, 'the wilderness' describes both the geographical location and Elijah's emotional state.

So what happened next? God, in the presence of an angel, provided sustenance and took Elijah even further into the desert—to the site of the holy mountain of revelation (called Sinai or Horeb). Alone, on the side of the mountain, Elijah has things to learn from God. At first it is Elijah who talks, telling God of the people's rejection of the covenant and the threat to his life. After listening, God tells Elijah to wait on the mountain.

In succession, Elijah experiences a great and powerful wind that shatters the rocks, an earthquake, and a fire—all manifestations of nature at its most terrible and dramatic, and all symbolic of Elijah's turbulent emotions and fears. Yet, contrary to expectation, God is in none of these phenomena. Finally, it is the contrasting sound of a gentle whisper that Elijah recognises as the authentic voice of God. His response is to hide his face, as Moses did, lest he inadvertently looks on God (19:9–13; Exodus 3:6).

If Elijah's motivation for entering the desert was to flee, once he was there God showed his love by ministering to his needs and leading him to the place of revelation. When revelation occurred, however, it was not because of the might, grandeur or majesty of the location; it was the silence that allowed him to hear.

'When you pray, you yourself must be silent; let the prayer speak'
(Orthodox saying).

NICK READ

Jesus in the wilderness

Then Jesus was led by the Spirit into the wilderness to be tempted by the devil. After fasting for forty days and forty nights, he was hungry. The tempter came to him and said, 'If you are the Son of God, tell these stones to become bread.' Jesus answered, 'It is written, "Man shall not live on bread alone, but on every word that comes from the mouth of God."'

The New Testament offers the perspective that Jesus, in person, emulates the people of Israel in their wilderness journeys. As the Israelites were led by God on their journey through the desert, so Jesus is also led by God into the desert. Matthew's and Luke's Gospels both state that Jesus was 'led by the Spirit' into the desert (see Luke 4:1), whilst Mark 1:12 asserts that 'the Spirit sent him out into the desert' (Mark 1:12). The parallel is meant to be drawn between the 40 days of Jesus' experience and the 40 years of Israel's wanderings.

As we shall see on Tuesday, Israel's wilderness experiences were designed to teach them 'that man does not live on bread alone but on every word that comes from the mouth of the Lord' (Deuteronomy 8:3). However, when Jesus faced the same experience, he didn't need to be taught the lesson. His response showed that he already embodied that understanding, as he quoted from the book of Deuteronomy.

This is a sign of encouragement as we undergo our own wilderness experiences. It has always been the Christian belief that Christ understands our temptations and shares our perils, but also that he is the exemplar and guide in all that we do and that he will lead us to triumph. Jesus in the desert shows us another example of the Saviour who shares human experience to the full and who therefore is able to 'feel sympathy for our weaknesses', and has been 'tempted in every way', yet 'did not sin' (Hebrews 4:15).

'O God our Father, hear me, who am trembling in this darkness, and stretch forth thy hand unto me; hold forth thy light before me; recall me from my wanderings; and, thou being my guide, may I be restored to myself and to thee' (Augustine, AD354–430).

NICK READ

Sharing the lessons of wilderness

For I do not want you to be ignorant of the fact, brothers and sisters, that our ancestors were all under the cloud and that they all passed through the sea. They were all baptised into Moses in the cloud and in the sea. They all ate the same spiritual food and drank the same spiritual drink; for they drank from the spiritual rock that accompanied them, and that rock was Christ. Nevertheless, God was not pleased with most of them; their bodies were scattered in the wilderness. Now these things occurred as examples to keep us from setting our hearts on evil things as they did.

Israel's wilderness experience was for our benefit as well as theirs. The exodus and the wilderness wonderings are understood by Paul to be an analogy of Christian experience. Paul draws out the parallels in his letter here: as we are baptised in Christ, so the people of Israel shared a baptism into the fellowship of Moses; as we share in the Eucharist, so the people of Israel shared in their own spiritual food and drink; as we are guided by God, so they were guided and protected by the cloud. In fact, it is ultimately the same rock, Christ, that accompanied both them and us and from which we all draw sustenance.

Yet their reaction was often of complaint and rebellion, leading to their judgement and the continuation of their wilderness experience for 40 years until the rebellious generation had been scattered in the desert. It was a barrier to their inheritance of the promised land. Paul is anxious that his readers do not commit the same mistakes or foster the same response, and that we both understand and benefit from the lessons of our shared history.

'Deliver me, O God, from a slothful mind, from all lukewarmness, and all dejection of spirit. I know these cannot but deaden my love to thee; mercifully free my heart from them, and give me a lively, zealous, active and cheerful spirit; that I may vigorously perform whatever thou commandest, thankfully suffer whatever thou choosest for me, and be ever ardent to obey in all things thy holy love' (John Wesley, 1703–91).

NICK READ

Wilderness: learning to listen

Then Moses led Israel from the Red Sea and they went into the Desert of Shur. For three days they travelled in the desert without finding water. When they came to Marah, they could not drink its water because it was bitter. (That is why the place is called Marah.) So the people grumbled against Moses, saying, 'What are we to drink?' Then Moses cried out to the Lord, and the Lord showed him a piece of wood. He threw it into the water, and the water became fit to drink.

The wilderness of Shur is a portion of Sinai, east of Egypt. After three days without water, the weight of expectation must have been very high when water was finally found. However, the water was bitter and undrinkable (Marah means 'bitter'), and the lack of water led to grumbling and resentment, directed primarily against Moses. It was Moses alone who cried out to the Lord. The response from God was to show Moses a piece of wood which, when thrown into the water, made it sweet. The wood does not explain why the water became sweet, but the depth of the story lies in the contrast between the two responses to the situation—the response of bitterness, grumbling and resentment, or the response of one who seeks God.

The word translated 'showed' (v. 25) has the same root as the word for 'to instruct' or 'to teach', and is the key principle behind the Torah (the law) by which God instructs his people. When he turned to God, Moses received instruction which, when acted upon, turned bitter water into sweet. The lesson is brought out in the next few verses (16:25–27), in which this episode is conceived as a test, and a contrast is drawn between those who 'listen carefully to the voice of the Lord' and those who don't. The ultimate destination in the chapter is Elim, a place of pure water 'where there were twelve springs and seventy palm trees' (Exodus 15:27).

What 'bitter waters' are you aware of, that affect you or others?
Bring these concerns to God in prayer and keep an account of how
they are addressed by him.

NICK READ

Wilderness: learning to reflect

Remember how the Lord your God led you all the way in the wilderness these forty years, to humble and test you in order to know what was in your heart, whether or not you would keep his commands. He humbled you, causing you to hunger and then feeding you with manna, which neither you nor your ancestors had known, to teach you that man does not live on bread alone but on every word that comes from the mouth of God. Your clothes did not wear out and your feet did not swell during these forty years. Know then in your heart that as a man disciplines his son, so the Lord your God disciplines you.

The stress on the verbs 'humble' and 'test' suggests that the desert itinerary was a learning experience for Israel rather than a punishment. The Catholic theologian Raymond Brown posits that God had 'been good to them in the barren desert. They had learned lessons there which prosperity could never have taught them. Through those bleak wilderness years, he had been like a compassionate father who occasionally had to discipline his children for their own good. Some lessons can only be learnt in trouble.'

It was afterwards, when the Israelites had had time to reflect on their wilderness experience, that they understood how providential the time had been. We often want to escape from our wilderness experiences and, after escaping, leave the difficulties well behind, but there is value in remembering and taking time to prayerfully reflect on what we experienced and what we learnt of God. Israel's Psalms constantly reminded them how important the wilderness had been for their experience of God and their understanding of his love for them.

I bind unto myself today the power of God to hold and lead,
His eye to watch, his might to stay, his ear to hearken to my need.
The wisdom of my God to teach, his hand to guide, his shield to ward,
The word of God to give me speech, his heavenly host to be my guard.

From St Patrick's Breastplate'

NICK READ

Wilderness: learning to adapt

The Israelites left Rameses and camped at Sukkoth. They left Sukkoth and camped at Etham, on the edge of the desert. They left Etham, turned back to Pi Hahiroth, to the east of Baal Zephon, and camped near Migdol. They left Pi Hahiroth and passed through the sea into the desert, and when they had travelled for three days in the Desert of Etham, they camped at Marah. They left Marah and went to Elim, where there were twelve springs and seventy palm trees, and they camped there.

The litany of campsites in Numbers 33 stretches from verse 5 to verse 49. But that's the point: the children of Israel were constantly on the move, pitching and repitching their tents. In the 40 years they spent in the wilderness, they never arrived at the promised land; that fulfilment had to wait until Joshua became leader. This emphasis becomes more apparent in the Hebrew title for the book of Numbers, which is simply 'Bemidbar' or 'In the wilderness'.

But if they were constantly on the move, they also learned to adapt, and the wilderness began to shape their pattern of worship, not extinguish it. Every time they pitched camp, they prepared for God to dwell with them by erecting the tabernacle, or tent of meeting, which occupied the central place in the campsite. In Exodus 26 we find detailed instructions for the construction and erection of the tabernacle, which was designed as a prefabricated structure to be carried from site to site. The book of Leviticus is full of detailed instructions for how worship and sacrifice were to be conducted while on the move. These rituals didn't end because they were in the wilderness; the people adapted to the changing circumstances.

Wilderness experiences can drive change within our lives—and they are meant to do so. They provide us with opportunities to break out of familiar old patterns and embrace new ones, as long as we are minded to rise to the challenge and are not afraid of making mistakes.

What things are prompting change in your life? Are there opportunities to try new patterns of worship, prayer or praise in response?

NICK READ

Wilderness: learning to trust

He brought out Israel, laden with silver and gold, and from among their tribes no-one faltered. Egypt was glad when they left, because dread of Israel had fallen on them. He spread out a cloud as a covering, and a fire to give light at night. They asked, and he brought them quail; he fed the well with the bread of heaven. He opened the rock, and water gushed out; it flowed like a river in the desert. For he remembered his holy promise given to his servant Abraham.

The psalmist recounts the wilderness experience of Israel through rose-tinted spectacles in Psalm 105, in which God's faithfulness is matched by the people's faith and trust: 'among their tribes no-one faltered' (v. 37). The reality captured in the book of Numbers (and in the next psalm, Psalm 106) was rather different. Instead of demonstrating faith, the people complained bitterly and even suggested that death in Egypt would have been preferable to their current predicament (Numbers 14:2).

God did not give up on them, but it took time. It has been estimated that the journey from Egypt to Canaan could have been completed within eleven days, yet it actually took 40 years to teach the Israelites the lessons they needed to learn. But learn they did—that God was capable of sheltering, guiding and feeding them and that his reasons for doing so lay not in their wayward faithfulness, but in the promise that God had given to Abraham: 'I will make you into a great nation and I will bless you' (Genesis 12:2).

The emphasis of Psalm 105 is that what God does, he does handsomely. He spread out a cloud as a covering to protect the whole nation from the power of the sun, and gave a light to lead them throughout the blackest night. He brought miraculous food, the manna or 'bread of heaven'. Water didn't just trickle to slake their thirst, it positively gushed 'like a river'. It may have been a tough environment in which to learn, but eventually the lessons stuck.

What experiences require your trust in God? How easy do you find this, and what lessons are you learning?

NICK READ

Wilderness: learning tenacity

You, God, are my God, earnestly I seek you; I thirst for you, my whole being longs for you, in a dry and parched land where there is no water. I have seen you in the sanctuary and beheld your power and your glory. Because your love is better than life, my lips will glorify you. I will praise you as long as I live, and in your name I will lift up my hands. I will be satisfied as with the richest of foods; with singing lips my mouth will praise you. On my bed I remember you; I think of you through the watches of the night.

This psalm's superscription is 'A Psalm of David. When he was in the Desert of Judah.' David is in the desert, fleeing for his life from his son, Absalom, who has instigated a revolt (2 Samuel 15). Situated to the east of the Judean hills and sloping down to the Dead Sea, the Desert of Judah is depicted as a dry and thirsty land. David's distress is palpable: both body and soul are in need of God. His predicament is a stark contrast to the happier times when he worshipped God in the sanctuary in Jerusalem.

But David's response to this situation was not despair but faith. Even in the desert he was prepared to glorify God and lift his hands in worship. The wilderness sharpened, not diminished, his appetite for God. If he experienced sleeplessness, then he would pray through 'the watches of the night' (a phrase that suggests the slow progress of the hours). The word translated 'remember' (v. 6) is the same word found in Psalm 1:2, about the man who 'meditates' on the law of the Lord day and night.

The contrast being drawn is between a soul that is thirsting for God (v. 1) and a soul that will be satisfied with the richest of foods (v. 5). Although that satisfaction was far removed from the reality of David's current situation, rather than becoming resigned to his fate he chose to resign his fate to the Lord.

'You, God, are my God, earnestly I seek you.'

NICK READ

Wilderness: learning to pray

Then his people recalled the days of old, the days of Moses and his people—where is he who brought them through the sea, with the shepherd of his flock? Where is he who set his Holy Spirit among them, who sent his glorious arm of power to be at Moses' right hand, who divided the waters before them, to gain for himself everlasting renown, who led them through the depths? Like a horse in open country, they did not stumble; like cattle that go down to the plain, they were given rest by the Spirit of the Lord. This is how you guided your people to make for yourself a glorious name.

This passage from Isaiah 63 has been described by Alec Motyer as the actions of a 'remembrancer at prayer', one of the watchman appointed by God whose purpose was to call upon the Lord until God's promises were fulfilled (Isaiah 62:6–7). The prayer is rooted in the recollection of Israel's experience in the wilderness. It is a lamentation, a reminder to the hearer of how close they were to God during that experience, but also a pointed reminder, directed towards God, that his reputation will for ever be associated with the welfare of his people.

The purpose of the prayer is both to bring hope to the people and to stir God into action. How could the God who did all those things—who brought them through the sea, who set his Holy Spirit among them, who sent his glorious arm of power and divided the waters—not continue to demonstrate his love for his people? This prayer is a sustained review of God's faithfulness, in order to ask more of God in the future.

There are lots of instances in the Bible that show the wilderness as a geographical setting in which people pray, including Jesus' own prayers, as we saw last week. But wilderness is also the basis for our prayers to God. Whatever our experiences or our failings, we should never cease to ask of God.

Although the wilderness is tough, take time to thank God for these experiences in our lives as we grow in faith.

NICK READ

Lamentations

'All our enemies have opened their mouths against us; panic and pitfall have come upon us, devastation and destruction. My eyes flow with rivers of tears because of the destruction of my people' (Lamentations 3:46–48, NRSV).

Lamentations is not easy to read. Unlike many of the other books in the Bible, which describe a deepening awareness of God's presence and a journey towards an affirmed and mature faith, this tells the story of a dark period in Israel's history. Jerusalem has fallen, the temple has been destroyed and the people are in mourning for all that they have lost.

To journey through Lamentations is to accept what it is to be human, fallible and vulnerable. As we travel alongside a people shocked, saddened and in despair, we recognise that we too know those feelings, even if at times we try to hide them. In the pain and distress of others, we can learn more about ourselves—how our faith can sometimes feel fragile, our belief stretched almost to breaking point.

We might read Lamentations today as a diary of what it is like to live with depression after trauma. The author is sad, lonely and isolated from sources of help and support. There are physical symptoms as well as mental distress, and a lack of interest in the things that formerly gave pleasure. Shame, denial and anger lead to attempts to bargain with God, and then to withdrawal and depression. Finally, there is acceptance of the situation as it is and the tiniest glimmer of hope for the future.

The book does not come to a neat conclusion, because it describes a situation that is still in progress. Our lives are like that too; in the middle of events, whether good or bad, it is impossible to have the perspective that comes with time and distance. If Lamentations teaches us anything, it is that sometimes all we can do is hold on, even if—especially if—it seems impossible to do so. God is still with us despite our doubts.

Lamentations ends before there is a turning point, but catastrophe, through God's grace, does not have to be the end. In times of trouble, we too can cry out, 'Remember us, O Lord!' We will be heard.

AMANDA BLOOR

Abandonment

How lonely sits the city that once was full of people! How like a widow she has become, she that was great among the nations! She that was a princess among the provinces has become a vassal. She weeps bitterly in the night, with tears on her cheeks; among all her lovers she has no one to comfort her; all her friends have dealt treacherously with her, they have become her enemies.

How important are friendships to you? Some people are able to be quietly self-contained, but, for many, the support of others is crucial to their well-being. Whether we seek encouragement in the company of a few individuals who have known us for many years, through colleagues or those who share our leisure interests, or in vast numbers of virtual 'friends' whom we meet only online, it's easy to judge our self-worth by the affirmation we receive from others.

How difficult it is, then, if that friendship is withdrawn or if those whom we trusted let us down! Suddenly, our world shifts and we are unsure of who we are. If we feel alone and lonely, friendless, betrayed and without comfort, it is easy to fall into despair, weeping in the night and believing that the whole world is against us.

This is when we most need God, although in the depths of misery it can be difficult to recognise the divine presence. Perhaps, we might think, we deserve this experience. Perhaps God has abandoned us too and we are quite alone.

If we look to the world to discover who we are, we can be deceived. Like the hall of mirrors at a fairground, the image that the world reflects back to us can be partial, distorted or unbalanced. We need to look instead to the God in whose image we are made and who loves us still.

Creator God, help us to hold on to the knowledge that you love all that you have made. When despair threatens to overwhelm us, give us grace to trust that you are with us in the darkest night. Fill us with hope and bring us back into the daylight of your presence.

AMANDA BLOOR

Disinterest

The roads to Zion mourn, for no one comes to the festivals; all her gates are desolate, her priests groan; her young girls grieve, and her lot is bitter.

Even the roads of the city are in mourning and its gates are desolated. The fate that has afflicted Zion is of such magnitude that the structures built to lead travellers towards the city and to keep its people safe are now symbols of failure that seem to have absorbed misery as a sponge absorbs water. It is not only the priests and young girls who groan and grieve; the very architecture that had been a reflection of power, glory and confidence has become a mockery of human endeavour.

When disaster strikes, it's very easy to stop taking an interest in anything at all. A classic sign of depression is the inability to engage with things that would previously have given pleasure. Enthusiasm is replaced by an overwhelming sense of lethargy and exhaustion. Everything is too much effort and seems, ultimately, worthless.

We are told in this passage that no one comes to the religious festivals any more. The residents of the city, as well as the visitors drawn from further afield, have given up on worship and celebration. Perhaps they are afraid to gather together, apprehensive of even worse to come, or perhaps they simply can't see the point. Yet it's important to note the implication that the festivals are still continuing. Somewhere, someone is holding fast to the old traditions and to the faith that underpins them.

If we find ourselves in a time of sorrow or trial, we can forget to do the very things that sustain us. Prayer and worship might not be easy when we are troubled, but they keep us focused upon God. Even if it feels like going through the motions, keeping touch with faith can be a lifeline.

Lord Jesus Christ, help me to remember that you too felt isolated, rejected and alone. You walked towards the cross despite the knowledge of suffering ahead. Walk with me in times of sorrow and show me that there is hope.

AMANDA BLOOR

Precious things

Jerusalem remembers, in the days of her affliction and wandering, all the precious things that were hers in days of old. When her people fell into the hand of the foe, and there was no one to help her, the foe looked on mocking over her downfall.

How tempting it is, when times are hard, to look back! And how difficult it is, when doing so, to keep a sense of balance. When Jerusalem remembers the 'precious' things that she possessed, they are contrasted with her situation now. She is a wanderer, without safety or security, and is mocked by her enemies. Her people are no longer free and she has no sources of help. There's a note of self-pity: 'That is what I was in the past; how can I have been reduced to this?'

I wonder what the 'precious things' were for which Jerusalem mourned. We have seen, sadly, plenty of examples in recent years of people being forced out of their homes and their countries. Photographs of refugees fleeing from danger often show people bowed under mountains of possessions, crammed into overloaded cars or pushing precariously balanced wheelbarrows. What would you take with you if you had to leave home suddenly? Cash? Cooking utensils? Blankets? Or perhaps the irreplaceable items that sum up your past—photographs, souvenirs, a pair of baby shoes, a note from a loved one?

Yet after a while, these possessions become weight that has to be discarded or let go. Children need carrying, food is more important than jewels, and prayer may be the only freedom that remains. In times of extremity, life is stripped down to its essentials.

Is Jerusalem mourning for the fripperies and luxuries of the past, the things that gave her status, or has she learned what is really important? What are the 'precious things' in your life that you would want to protect and keep with you?

God of our journeying, guide us through times of difficulty and sustain us when we have to let go of the past. Help us to recognise what really matters, so that we are able to look with confidence to a better future.

AMANDA BLOOR

Being shamed

Jerusalem sinned grievously, so she has become a mockery; all who honoured her despise her, for they have seen her nakedness; she herself groans, and turns her face away.

The sexual imagery and gendered language used in this passage are uncomfortable to modern ears. There is a shift from describing Jerusalem as 'daughter Zion' (v. 6), which sounds affectionate and gives her an honoured position within God's family, to a cold condemnation of her sinful behaviour, exposing her to the gaze of those who now despise her. Is it her nakedness that is the source of her shame, I wonder, or has she been figuratively or literally stripped in front of her critics, revealed and humbled? Does she groan from shame, or because she feels misused?

There are parallels, of course, with contemporary public figures and the fickleness of rapidly moving communications media that build people up—often through notoriety—and then appear to delight in bringing them back down. Entertainment is all, and 'being famous', no matter what for, becomes an end in itself. Young people in particular are discovering that a moment of foolishness, once documented online, can quickly spread to an audience of unimaginable size, leaving them devastated and horrified by the consequences.

Which of us, I wonder, has not at some time done something of which we are ashamed? We are human and fallible, so prone to making mistakes. But our response to our own errors of judgement or the errors of others can expose fault-lines in our relationship with God and our sense of dignity as children of God. Is it easier to forgive others than to forgive ourselves? Does our behaviour drive other people away, and do we find ourselves turning, in shame, away from God? And do we really believe that it is possible for us to sin so grievously that God would abandon us?

Gracious God, who offers forgiveness to all who repent, help us to remember that our faith is built upon resurrection and that you will never leave us. Through your generosity, lead us into the future won for us by Christ, our past left behind and new life ahead.

AMANDA BLOOR

Sharing the weight

My transgressions were bound into a yoke; by his hand they were fastened together; they weigh on my neck, sapping my strength; the Lord handed me over to those whom I cannot withstand.

We sometimes talk about being weighed down by cares, and if you look at someone who is anxious or unhappy, their body often reflects it. They are physically bowed down; head drooping, shoulders hunched, eyes lowered. There is a tenseness about them, muscles held tightly as if fighting against an unseen burden.

Here the city speaks with a victim's voice. Handed over to those who are stronger than she, there is no possibility of escape from her fate; she is unable to stand against those who punish her. She blames herself for what has happened: her own wrongdoings have been laid on her shoulders. Like many victims, she believes that what has befallen her is her own fault.

Guilt is horrible. It is corrosive, eating away at self-belief and dignity. The knowledge of sinfulness is a burden that is too heavy to bear, and it is easy to sink under its weight. Yet we do not have to carry this load alone. Remember that Christ described his yoke, unlike the yoke of punishment described in this passage, as 'easy' and 'light' (Matthew 11:30); he effectively offers to share our burdens, taking the weight of them from our shoulders.

This is not to negate the seriousness of sin. Guilt, once recognised, can be the beginning of a reshaping of one's life. It can cause us to stop, take stock and repent. But it is important not to get stuck in the trap of self-loathing that imprisons and exhausts us until we can see no way out. Jesus shows a better way and can help us to stand tall, freed from the burdens placed upon our shoulders by others or by our own transgressions.

Lord Jesus Christ, you had to carry the weight of the cross. Help me not to sink under my own burdens or to be afraid to turn to you. With your aid, let me stand upright again.

AMANDA BLOOR

Lashing out

All my enemies heard of my trouble; they are glad that you have done it. Bring on the day you have announced, and let them be as I am. Let all their evildoing come before you; and deal with them as you have dealt with me because of all my transgressions; for my groans are many and my heart is faint.

Those of us who have siblings, or have had contact with young children, will recognise that aggrieved cry: 'It's not fair!' Whatever the offence, great or small, that has caused a perceived injustice, there is an instant appeal for the offender to be recognised and punished, especially if the accuser has themselves been reprimanded for the same actions.

We might hope that we leave childish responses behind as we reach adulthood, but most of us can point to moments when we wished speedy retribution upon others or felt that we were being singled out for chastisement when others had behaved similarly. Whether at work or at home, we still have the capacity to metaphorically stamp our feet and roar out, 'Tell them off too!'

How much is this response due to an innate desire for the world to be an orderly place, where justice reigns and all people are treated equally, and how much due to the desire to shift responsibility from our own actions by blaming others? If they have also behaved badly, then focusing attention on them removes the spotlight from our own failings.

Much as parents see through the clumsy strategies of their children, God knows our motives better than we admit to ourselves. It's easy to call down punishment on another in the hope that this will make us feel better, but it's a tactic that's unlikely to work. Instead, we are commanded to forgive, to turn the other cheek and take responsibility for our actions. It's the first step towards maturity and growth.

I feel let down, Lord, when I am in trouble and others flourish despite their wrongdoing. Help me to turn to you, sorry for what I have done, confident that you will help me learn from it, and trusting that you love me still.

AMANDA BLOOR

Shoring up the ruins

The Lord has destroyed without mercy all the dwellings of Jacob; in his wrath he has broken down the strongholds of daughter Judah; he has brought down to the ground in dishonour the kingdom and its rulers.

We live in a society that prizes house ownership as a sign of permanence, stability and financial acuity. Our homes are thought to reflect something of who we are; living in a 'desirable' area, having good taste in interior décor, furnishing kitchens and living rooms with the latest gadgets and technology—all are seen as clues to our social standing and our ability to create something that will impress others. But for many, owning their own home is not an option. Personal circumstances, finances, family requirements or the demands of work can make it impossible or foolish for them to buy a house.

As we see in this passage, the security offered by bricks and mortar can be illusory. The city has been brought to ruin, its strongholds and dwellings destroyed and its rulers shamed and dishonoured. The walls that looked so strong and provided safe shelter have become the target of the enemy, drawing attention and danger. From the most wealthy to the poorest, Zion's citizens have learned that they are vulnerable after all. Their homes have not been able to save them.

History shows us again and again that human defences are not, in the end, impregnable. Strongholds, kingdoms and rulers will all fall at some point. Throughout the ages, towns and cities have been brought to rubble and their inhabitants made homeless, forced to find shelter where they can and to search for a place of safety and welcome.

There is only one way in which we can find the security that we crave. Earthly kingdoms falter, but the heavenly kingdom endures. Can we become builders and work to create God's kingdom here on earth?

God of our refuge, be for us a source of shelter when the world threatens to overwhelm us. Be our place of defence and safety, and make us builders of a better world, inspired by your Spirit and filled with your love.

AMANDA BLOOR

Documenting horror

The elders of daughter Zion sit on the ground in silence; they have thrown dust on their heads and put on sackcloth; the young girls of Jerusalem have bowed their heads to the ground. My eyes are spent with weeping.

During World War I, doctors were bewildered by the number of soldiers who, after spending time on the front line, under bombardment and in fear of their lives, simply came to a halt. Their bodies refused to function normally, they were emotionally unstable, and some of them became unable to see, hear or speak. Initially called 'shell shock' and thought to be a physical reaction caused by proximity to explosions (or cruelly dismissed as 'malingering'), the condition was discovered to be a psychological reaction to trauma as overburdened minds retreated from horror.

Recent conflicts have reminded us of the emotional price paid by the victims of war. Charities work to rehabilitate child soldiers, brutalised by the atrocities they have been forced to commit; women and girls who have been grievously misused by the enemy often find themselves rejected by their own communities, tainted by the abuse that they have suffered. When life as you have known it comes to an end, there are no easy solutions and few happy outcomes.

Sometimes, as we see in this passage, it is impossible to say or do anything in response to outrageous events. The elderly sit silently, dust and sackcloth symbolising their mourning for what has happened, while young women look down to the ground, uninterested in what goes on around them. They have passed into the state of emotional exhaustion that follows extreme sorrow; there are, quite literally, no more tears to shed.

It can be impossible to find adequate words to describe horror and suffering, and facile to try. Perhaps all we can do is to document what has happened, refusing to turn away—and pray.

Lord, sometimes I hear the news and feel sick at heart. We are capable of such cruelty to each other. When I feel that there is nothing I can do, remind me to love others, being rooted and grounded in you.

AMANDA BLOOR

Who is trustworthy?

Your prophets have seen for you false and deceptive visions; they have not exposed your iniquity to restore your fortunes, but have seen oracles for you that are false and misleading.

If we feel vulnerable, it can be tempting to surround ourselves with individuals whose encouragement will bolster our self-image. We can seek out people who will say only nice things, avoiding those who know us well and can be uncomfortably direct. Sometimes it's hard to tell who our real friends are and whether what we are being told is the truth or simply what we wish to hear.

Recent television and stage shows have featured illusionists who amaze audiences by their ability to read minds, perform astounding feats, influence individuals and do tricks that are apparently impossible. We know, of course, that they are not doing 'magic' but are experts in sleight of hand, misdirection and recognising the subliminal signals given out through body language. We realise that we are being manipulated, and we enjoy suspending disbelief for the sake of entertainment.

Sadly, the same skills and techniques can be used by fraudsters with intent to deceive. Whether it's the email purporting to seek investors for a sure business opportunity, or the pickpocket creating a diversion and relieving the unwary of their wallets, the combination of dishonest intent and psychological acuity can leave victims feeling gullible and ashamed.

After the devastation of Zion, it must have been easy for false prophets to interpret events and give advice about the future. No doubt they had reasons to do so: power, influence and financial gain can be strong motivating forces. Yet their visions and oracles were based upon deceit rather than truth, and they offered false comfort. How is a better future to be built if the reasons for the current situation are not addressed? A good friend may speak truth that can be painful, but truth spoken in love is the bearer of hope rather than falsehood.

Holy Spirit, Wisdom of God, help me to set aside self-deception and turn towards what is right and good, through Jesus Christ, who is the way, the life and the truth.

AMANDA BLOOR

Crying out

Arise, cry out in the night, at the beginning of the watches! Pour out your heart like water before the presence of the Lord! Lift your hands to him for the lives of your children, who faint for hunger at the head of every street.

Many of us were encouraged as children to be brave and 'keep a stiff upper lip'. It was seen as self-indulgent to make a fuss or to complain, so tears were choked back and tempers kept under control as we learned appropriate behaviour. I wonder, if this was your experience, how it affects your relationship with God. It is quite possible that you see God as a parent who is to be impressed by your stoicism in the face of adversity, and who might be displeased if you were to express unhappiness or negativity.

Of course, each of us can think of times in life when we have been made angry or upset by circumstances beyond our control. Although we might be wary of admitting those feelings, even to ourselves, it is likely that we are better able to express fury or hurt on behalf of others, especially the most vulnerable—the very young, the old or the infirm.

Sometimes we need to be given permission to be furious. Here, we are shown Zion being encouraged to speak out on behalf of her children, who are starving and near to death. 'Cry out!' she is told; 'pour out your heart like water' and raise your hands in appeal to God. The situation is desperate; there is no point in holding back.

God is someone with whom it is completely safe to express our deepest feelings. All healthy relationships depend upon honesty and trust, and our relationship with the Creator is no different. To attempt to hide how we feel turns us from close members of God's family into polite strangers.

Are there things you would like to say to God, that you have suppressed? If so, open your heart in prayer. God is always willing to listen.

Dear God, sometimes situations fill me with fury or pain. Help me to cry out, knowing that you are always ready to hear me.

AMANDA BLOOR

Blocks and barriers

[God] has walled me about so that I cannot escape; he has put heavy chains on me; though I call and cry for help, he shuts out my prayer; he has blocked my ways with hewn stones, he has made my paths crooked.

People suffering from depression sometimes describe the experience as like being locked into a prison cell. It's as if walls are closing in, darkness is encroaching and there is no way out. It can feel like a life sentence for a crime that you didn't commit.

There are always times in the Christian life when our relationship with God falters. If we are able to pray, we feel that our prayers are not getting through. When we beg for help from God, we cannot see that there is a response. Wherever we turn, whatever we do, life seems difficult and complex, with endless obstacles in our path. It's easy to believe that we are being punished, to become bitter or to pretend that we don't care. If God has let us down, then what do we need of God?

This is the time to ask yourself, difficult as it may be, 'Is it possible that I have built barriers to keep God away?' When we are sad, disappointed or angry, we can push away the people who love us. We can't risk being further hurt, and so we shut them out just at the moment when we need them most.

Yet if we are able to hold on to the smallest chink of light, we know that freedom will come. We will escape from the prison walls that have surrounded us and threatened to crush our spirit. And we will look back and realise that God was, all the time, alongside us in our distress.

God of our future and our past, you see the road that lies ahead of us. When we stumble and fall, pick us up and encourage us onwards. Grant us glimpses of your presence, even when we refuse to look for you; and, through Christ's love, break down the walls that oppress and enclose us.

AMANDA BLOOR

Remembering the past

I called on your name, O Lord, from the depths of the pit; you heard my plea, 'Do not close your ear to my cry for help, but give me relief!' You came near when I called on you; you said, 'Do not fear!'

We've thought about how difficult it can be to believe that we will be escape from the things that bind and oppress us. Whether we are trapped by physical, mental or spiritual issues, it is easy, even when calling upon God, to think that nothing will change. Yet faith knows differently.

Here we see one of the rare chinks of light in the book of Lamentations. A few verses earlier (3:40), Israel decided to 'return to the Lord', and now there is a determined attempt to recall the good moments of the former relationship between the people and God. It reads almost like the therapy sessions of a couple whose marriage has been under stress, who have been instructed to describe positive things about their partner.

At this unspecified time, God hears the cries of despair and comes near, offering encouragement: 'Don't be afraid!' This is one of the most frequently occurring phrases in the Bible, and it is exactly what is needed at this point. There are no easy words offering a swift solution, no attempts to minimise the pain of what has occurred, but the simple comfort of a loving presence. 'I am with you. Do not fear.'

Can you recognise a moment in your life when you called out for help and recognised the divine presence? God is revealed to us in a variety of ways, so for each person this experience will be different, but it can be something so meaningful that it is never forgotten. Hold on to it, know that it was true, and believe what it shows you: there is hope; the darkness will come to an end; God never gives up.

Help me, Lord, not to forget your goodness to me. In times of trouble, let me remember that I knew your closeness once. Give me the grace to trust that I will know it again.

AMANDA BLOOR

Living in hell

Now their visage is blacker than soot; they are not recognised in the streets. Their skin has shrivelled on their bones; it has become as dry as wood. Happier were those pierced by the sword that those pierced by hunger, whose life drains away, deprived of the produce of the field. The hands of compassionate women have boiled their own children; they became their food in the destruction of my people.

This is a truly nightmarish vision. Famine resulting from warfare has devastated the land, and its people are reduced to desperate measures. Formerly sleek, well fed and richly clothed, the rich are unrecognisable as they waste away, burned by the sun, their skin shrunken, dirty and brittle from neglect and hunger. It would have been better, they believe, to have died quickly from the swift stab of the enemy's sword than to endure the endless pangs of starvation, life gradually ebbing away.

Yet there is even worse—hard to hear and almost impossible to imagine. Formerly caring mothers have taken to cannibalism, cooking the bodies of their children in a desperate attempt to cling to life and perhaps to sustain the stronger members of their families. This is a great sin, provoking God's fury, and the ultimate taboo. How far the people have fallen!

It can be easy, when we see the sins of others, to believe complacently that we would never be reduced to such behaviour. There are lines that we think, or hope, we would never cross. Yet who can tell how they might react when provoked or in the most challenging of circumstances?

The Lord's Prayer asks that we should not be brought to the time of trial. Pray that you never find yourself facing situations where you are tempted to commit sin, and pray that those who have done terrible things may turn to God in supplication and repentance.

Jesus Christ, our brother and our friend, you faced temptation but clung to God in prayer. Help us, in times of trial, to find our strength in you, and grant us compassion for those who are tested beyond their endurance.

AMANDA BLOOR

Living in uncertainty

Why have you forgotten us completely? Why have you forsaken us these many days? Restore us to yourself, O Lord, that we may be restored; renew our days as of old—unless you have utterly rejected us, and are angry with us beyond measure.

If the book of Lamentations were a novel or a fairy story, we would be hoping for a happy ending. We like loose ends tied up, the future hopeful and all uncertainty removed. Unfortunately, real life is not always like that, and this book ends on a sad note. The city still lies desolate, its people are still hungry and terrible punishments have been inflicted upon young and old alike.

After the fury and emotion of the earlier text, this passage seems strangely subdued. Instead of roaring aloud to God and demanding rescue, there is a quiet simplicity here. 'Why have you forgotten us, leaving us to face this alone?' they ask. 'Have we gone so far astray that you have left us?' There seems no point in trying to bargain with God or continuing to express denial or anger about the situation. Instead, there is an uneasy acceptance that this is how things are and that change might not come.

When we are caught in the middle of difficult or dreadful events, it can be almost impossible to foresee a time when things will be better. Our focus is on what is happening at this particular moment, right in front of us. But God, unlike us, is able to see the bigger picture.

It might not be possible for us to feel hopeful in dire situations, and certainly, for the author of Lamentations there is at this point no sense of future promise. Yet there is the smallest glimmer of possibility in the appeal to God. When all else fails and our strength is gone, all we can do is to cast ourselves on God's mercy and pray that we too 'may be restored'.

Loving God, when all hope is exhausted and the future looks bleak, help me to turn to you. You are all that I can cling to. Restore me to yourself, Lord, that I may carry on.

AMANDA BLOOR

Angels

It was seven in the morning, before I had activated my brain with the first cup of tea, when my seven-year-old granddaughter demanded to know, 'Is heaven real, Grandma?' In hindsight, I should have simply replied, 'What do you think?' but, not being fully conscious, I tried to offer a few answers: 'Well, it's not a place, more like a state of being...' and 'Perhaps we can make heaven here on earth, depending on how we live our lives.' Neither of these responses seemed to impress her very much.

Now, as I reflect with you for a week on 'angels', I wonder whether she might, any day soon, ask me, 'Are angels real, Grandma?' How would I respond? Perhaps I would invite her, as I now invite you, to ponder, 'What do you think?'

An American film, *City of Angels*, opens with a scene in a hospital in Los Angeles, which means 'the angels'. We are aware of various beings there who look like ordinary mortals but have an air of deep serenity about them. We soon realise that they are especially present to people at the extremes of life—for example, at birth, at death and at times of severe pain, danger or need. To others, they seem to be invisible.

My own sense of angels is very much like that. They usually appear as ordinary human beings who seem to be imbued with a loving and holy spirit and a presence that transcends normal mortal expectations. They appear at times of need, when we are afraid or troubled or heading into danger without realising it. They move through our lives unexpectedly, and scripture reminds us of the importance of generous hospitality towards the stranger, 'for by doing that some have entertained angels without knowing it' (Hebrews 13:2).

This week we approach the season when the angels sing their Hosannas across a weary world to announce the coming of a new story—a love story, a story with the potential to change the world, embodied in a newborn infant in an unregarded corner of the Middle East.

Whatever angels mean to you, they are the heralds of divine love. This week's reflections invite you to consider the ways in which they may have become real for you.

MARGARET SILF

Visiting angels

The Lord appeared to Abraham by the oaks of Mamre, as he sat at the entrance of his tent in the heat of the day. He looked up and saw three men standing near him. When he saw them, he ran from the tent entrance to meet them, and bowed down to the ground. He said, 'My lord, if I find favour with you, do not pass by your servant. Let a little water be brought, and wash your feet, and rest yourselves under the tree. Let me bring a little bread, that you may refresh yourselves.'

Abraham's encounter with the three messengers of God by the oaks of Mamre has been immortalised in Andrei Rublev's icon of the Trinity, which is seen to represent not only Abraham's three angelic guests but also the holy Trinity itself.

Middle Eastern hospitality is legendary, the poorest of families often setting their choicest food before guests while going hungry themselves. Abraham is no exception. He and Sarah unhesitatingly bring the angelic visitors all that hospitality demands, beginning with water to refresh themselves and leading to a feast, not merely of bread but, as the passage goes on to relate, of calf meat, curds and milk.

This is desert country. Bread and water mean life, and the angels do not depart without leaving Sarah and Abraham with their own gift of life. Sarah, long past childbearing age, is to bear a son who will bring blessings to all nations. The gift of life has been exchanged. Life engenders life in the unbroken circle that connects the angels in Rublev's icon.

It is said that the Western world is in the grip of a deadly epidemic called 'loneliness'. Far too many people today never see another human being, or engage in conversation, from one week's end to the next. Inwardly, they shrivel and die, and yet God's angels are at hand. A visit from a neighbour, an invitation to share a cup of tea or a friendly greeting in the street can bring the life-giving bread and water that tells them, 'I care.' And when this gift is offered, the giver invariably feels more alive too. Where life is given, life is returned, abundantly.

God is looking for visiting angels in your street. How might you respond?

MARGARET SILF

Connecting angels

Jacob left Beer-sheba and went towards Haran. He came to a certain place and stayed there for the night, because the sun had set. Taking one of the stones of the place, he put it under his head and lay down in that place. And he dreamed that there was a ladder set up on the earth, the top of it reaching to heaven; and the angels of God were ascending and descending on it.

After a major accident, Jennifer was left partially paralysed and confined to a wheelchair. Sadly, her husband, unable to cope with the new situation, left her. She struggled through life as best she could, greatly helped by the kindness and practical assistance of friends. One day, during a Quiet Day in her church, she was reflecting on how Jacob too found himself in a desolate place, with only a stone for a pillow, and yet, in that very place, encountered the angels of God ascending and descending the ladder that connected heaven and earth. At the end of the Quiet Day, Jennifer stunned us all with her heartfelt realisation, 'Surely God is in this stony place, and I never knew it' (see 28:16).

I have never been able to read about Jacob's ladder in quite the same way since that moment. Jennifer's discovery was no pious comment arising from the atmosphere of the day. It was a heartfelt 'Yes!' to the reality of her own experience. She knows too well the cruelty of those stones, but she also knows that the stony ground is the very place where the ladder begins, and that it rises straight into the very heart of holiness. She knows the angels, ascending and descending. They are the friends, and sometimes the strangers too, who keep on connecting her to God's love and compassion through their own simple acts of kindness.

When our lives go bad on us and God seems to be impossibly far away, somewhere there will be a ladder to remind us that the very place we stand is eternally connected to the heart of God, and there will be messengers sent to give us God's love in a thousand unexpected ways.

Have there been angels in your life who have reconnected you to God in your hours of need?

MARGARET SILF

Sustaining angels

[Elijah] went a day's journey into the wilderness, and came and sat down under a solitary broom tree. He asked that he might die: 'It is enough; now, O Lord, take away my life, for I am no better than my ancestors.' Then he lay down under the broom tree and fell asleep. Suddenly an angel touched him and said to him, 'Get up and eat.' He looked, and there at his head was a cake baked on hot stones, and a jar of water.

Most of us have known the feeling of being at the end of the line. There is simply no way forward, no energy left to fight the next battle, no motivation to keep going at all. We had such grand plans for a better world, and now, we realise, we are 'no better than our ancestors'. We are weary of it all and, like Elijah, all we want is to lie down and sleep—even to enter the final sleep for which Elijah begs.

Yet here we are, still going. Where did that energy come from? For Elijah, it came in the form of an angel and the simplest of meals—a cake and a jar of water. Not much for the long journey into the future, but enough to sustain the next few miles, reminding us that our life's journey is to be taken one small, trusting step at a time. Just as the people of Israel were sustained in the desert by a supply of food and water only ever sufficient for one day's journey, so it is for Elijah—and for us. Yet the sustaining love of the provider never runs out.

Sustaining angels cross our path more often than we realise, with their gentle invitations: 'Can I give you a hand?' 'May I help you carry that load?' 'Come in and rest a while.'

I once saw a pub advertising 'Free beer tomorrow, for everyone who missed it yesterday.' The world's promises are like that. Tomorrow never comes. The angel's message is different. With God it is always 'today', and there is always what we need for today's journey.

When did you last meet a sustaining angel? Can you be a sustaining angel for someone else?

MARGARET SILF

Announcing angels

In the sixth month the angel Gabriel was sent by God to a town in Galilee called Nazareth, to a virgin engaged to a man whose name was Joseph, of the house of David. The virgin's name was Mary. And he came to her and said, 'Greetings, favoured one! The Lord is with you... You will conceive in your womb and bear a son, and you will name him Jesus.'

I don't like interruptions. When I am engrossed in a book or watching a favourite TV programme, I don't appreciate it at all when the phone rings. I have often caught myself in these moments of irritated impatience, but one day my thoughts went a bit further and I found myself wondering how things would have been if Mary of Nazareth had been as intolerant of interruption as I am myself.

To describe the angel's visit as an 'interruption' in the smooth running of her young life is an enormous understatement. The angel's message would completely overthrow everything she had ever known or could possibly have expected. It would pitch her into a very unenviable situation that could easily have led to her death by stoning. But the angel didn't impose this future upon her. He offered it to her as a choice, held within a wholly reassuring affirmation of God's favour and love for her, and a promise of life—indeed, eternal life—within, and far beyond, what appeared to be a disastrous immediate prospect. She trusted the affirmation and the promise, as she made her historic response: 'Yes!'

Most of us will not have experienced circumstances so extreme or choices so demanding, but for us too there will have been times when some unwelcome interruption threatened to derail our carefully constructed life journeys. With hindsight, sometimes we can see the hand of God in these moments, especially if the interruption was challenging us to respond to something we knew was right but was nevertheless potentially disruptive. Mary of Nazareth is a model in so many ways—not least in the art of being open to interruptions, truly listening to the annunciations they may herald, and making the more life-giving choice in response.

May we be open to, and even welcome, interruptions.
They may be annunciations.

MARGARET SILF

Warning angels

Now after they had left, an angel of the Lord appeared to Joseph in a dream and said, 'Get up, take the child and his mother, and flee to Egypt, and remain there until I tell you; for Herod is about to search for the child, to destroy him.' Then Joseph got up, took the child and his mother by night, and went to Egypt, and remained there until the death of Herod.

Very often, when God is trying to get through to me, God has to make several attempts to penetrate the thick walls of my conscious mind before I get the message. Sometimes my conscious mind is completely impervious to anything the Holy Spirit might want to suggest to me. When this kind of fog has settled around me, I have found that the angels sometimes come, as they did to Joseph, in dreams.

Maybe you never remember your dreams, and maybe God doesn't have to storm the barricades of consciousness to get through to you. But for many people there are memories of what some might call 'deep dreams', that, in hindsight, appear to have been prophetic, profoundly affecting an important life choice. I have certainly had such dreams myself occasionally, and I am eternally grateful for the warnings they imparted. A friend of mine once dreamed that he had to cross a river. A little way upstream there was a large, elaborate bridge spanning the water. His dream seemed to suggest that he should choose to swim across rather than use the bridge. He struggled through the river, and was just about to reach the opposite bank when he looked back and saw that the bridge had collapsed.

Of course, only the dreamer knows what the dream means in practice for his or her own life, and only the dreamer can interpret the dream, through the Holy Spirit. Warning angels sometimes arrive when there is a real risk ahead, and they offer us warnings in symbols that our unconscious minds can grasp. If we listen to their wisdom, we will look back later and know that these warning angels were in fact guardian angels.

Has a warning angel ever visited your dreams in this way?
How did you respond?

MARGARET SILF

Consoling angels

Mary stood weeping outside the tomb. As she wept, she bent over to look into the tomb; and she saw two angels in white, sitting where the body of Jesus had been lying, one at the head and the other at the feet. They said to her, 'Woman, why are you weeping?' she said to them, 'They have taken away my Lord, and I do not know where they have laid him.' When she had said this, she turned round and saw Jesus.

Angels can be heard as well as seen. Debbie recently had to undergo a medical procedure that was causing her some anxiety. As she made the journey to the hospital with mounting apprehension, she noticed that familiar music was filling her mind. With her inner ear she was listening, quite unexpectedly, to Rutter's song 'The Lord bless you and keep you'—a musical angel. The more deeply she tuned in to this inner music, the calmer she became. When she finally arrived at the hospital, to her amazement and relief, she found an old friend sitting there, also awaiting a procedure. Like Mary, Debbie had been visited by two consoling angels that morning.

Another friend, Alison, died suddenly in the prime of life, leaving a distraught widower to mourn her. She wasn't 'religious' but she was deeply spiritual and had a great sense of humour. She had always promised, half in fun, that after she died she would return as a black butterfly. We had smiled at the time, but the smiles turned to tearful amazement at her funeral service. A black butterfly fluttered around the church, settling from time to time on various shoulders. After the service, everyone commented on it, but her husband, lost in sorrow like Mary, hadn't been aware of it. It was then that his second angel appeared, laid a friendly arm around his shoulders and consoled him: 'You see, Ron, Ali knew we all needed reassurance that she was there, but you didn't need an external sign, because she was and always will be at home in your heart.'

May we hear the angel voices that sing to us of God's love when we most need it, and may we be the angel voices to those who long to be consoled.

MARGARET SILF

Liberating angels

Then the high priest took action; he and all who were with him… being filled with jealousy, arrested the apostles and put them in the public prison. But during the night an angel of the Lord opened the prison doors, brought them out, and said, 'Go, stand in the temple and tell the people the whole message about this life.' When they heard this, they entered the temple at daybreak and went on with their teaching.

Prison bars can take many different forms, and so can angels. How might the apostles have felt that night, imprisoned by a hostile regime and dreading whatever might happen next? It was into this suffocating fog of terror that the liberating angel appeared, to open the prison doors.

Can angels, messengers of the Holy Spirit, penetrate our fears and set us free? Most surely they can, but they may not arrive with wings and harps. They may be so disguised that we fail to recognise them.

Jane, 85 years old and rather frail, lived alone in a district you wouldn't want to walk through after dark. One day she heard that her friend was in hospital. She knew she must visit, but that meant crossing some derelict land in the dark to get to the bus stop. Her fears escalated as she walked across this threatening landscape and saw four rather intimidating young men standing there in hoodies. She prayed for courage, faced her fears and approached them boldly, taking herself by surprise with her words: 'I'm glad you're here, lads. I was feeling a bit nervous on my own.' At this they became very protective: 'Don't you worry, granny. We'll take good care of you. No one will hurt you while we're here.'

Those angels were heavily disguised, but they set her free from the imprisonment of fear.

Liberation first frees us from something, but its full purpose is to free us for something. The apostles were freed from imprisonment, for a bold new ministry. The bus-stop angels freed Jane from her immediate fear, but through their response she was freed for something more—to be present to her friend lying alone in hospital.

What has imprisoned you in the past?
How, and for what, were you set free?

MARGARET SILF

John 1:1–14

Christmas is one of my favourite times of the year. Although I might joke about 'death by carol service', I genuinely enjoy (usually) each rendition of, for example, 'Away in a manger'. The people with whom I am singing are celebrating Jesus' arrival in the world, whatever the extent to which this is acknowledged ('yet the world did not know him', John 1:10). Meanwhile we have various services, meals and other activities during which we remember that 'the Word became flesh and lived among us' (v. 14) as we eat, drink, talk, laugh, give, receive and share in many different ways. The Christmas story is primarily about baby Jesus but the context is God's gift to God's world—then and now.

This year will be different for me. In recent months my father-in-law and my father have died and will be sadly missed during celebrations. The family homes where we spent many Christmases with those we love have been sold. More untimely has been the death, from a brain tumour, of a close friend and bridesmaid at our wedding; her funeral took place on what would have been her 31st birthday. Christmas for us, for that young woman's family and friends and for many people throughout the world will not be the tinsel-decked festival of Hollywood films. There will be a mixture of joy, sorrow, guilt, fear, hope and delight, feelings and memories both wanted and unwanted.

Perhaps this is a reason for reading slowly and pondering one of the most familiar 'seasonal' passages in the Bible. The opening verses of the Gospel of John are cosmic: the Word was God (v. 1). At the same time they are personal: the man's name was John (v. 6). During what can be a time of busyness and indulgence, attempting and failing to live an impossible dream of peace and goodwill to all, it is worth reflecting on the God who created the world, the God who knows individuals and can be known as one of us, the God who is the reason for the season. Whatever our personal circumstances, we might then gain perspective and have a new and life-giving experience of Christmas.

LAKSHMI JEFFREYS

In the beginning

In the beginning was the Word, and the Word was with God, and the Word was God. He was in the beginning with God.

The excitement would be palpable: 'We know this one and it's great!' So the first hearers of John's Gospel might have thought. 'In the beginning, God...' was as familiar to Jewish people as was 'the Word' (the Greek word *logos*) to anyone who read Greek in the ancient world. While, in the Old Testament, God created the whole world, day by day, feature by feature, the Greek *logos* was understood as the principle that shaped the universe. In the beginning there was creative activity. Something was going to happen—directed, planned and in the right order. This was something for philosophers and scientists alike.

What John does so beautifully is to take the much-loved, generally recognised opening words of the Hebrew scriptures and introduce a new element. In the beginning, at the moment of creation, the Word existed. The Word was in the presence of God the Father—uncreated, since the Word was God. This was not the impersonal 'word' of Greek philosophy. The one we know as Jesus was present at the start of everything—and it was this Word, this Jesus, who came to live among us. The cosmic Creator, the one who laughed, cried, taught and loved to death those among whom he lived; the God who knit you together in your mother's womb and painted the sky; the God who has loved you through whatever you have experienced in the past and will remain with you whatever happens in the future. The architect of the world is the baby in the crib.

Tomorrow, in many households around the world, something is going to happen—directed, planned and (everyone hopes) in the right order. The celebrations begin for millions of people today. In our church there will be crib services in the afternoon and a Communion service shortly before midnight. However you spend Christmas Eve, whether frantically busy or quietly waiting, perhaps you can make time to marvel at what happened in the very beginning.

God, who made everything, including you, has made himself known in the baby Jesus. How might this influence the beginning of your Christmas?

Christmas life

All things came into being through him, and without him not one thing came into being. What has come into being in him was life.

Happy Christmas! May Jesus bless you with life in all its fullness (John 10:10).

The Dog's Trust charity coined the phrase 'A dog is for life, not just for Christmas.' Thinking of the dog in our household, I am struck by how we shall love and care for her throughout her life. At the same time, she enhances our existence: our dog brings us life. Several church groups adapted the slogan: 'Jesus is for life, not just for Christmas.' Jesus is the way, the truth and the life (John 14:6), for the whole of our life and beyond.

The theme of 'life' occurs throughout John's Gospel. In Genesis, as we noted yesterday, the creative word of God was the source of life in the world. John echoes that in today's verses, but the subject is Jesus. Everything with life was created through Jesus. Some people consider a 'creative force' as a philosophical notion, but Jesus was a person. The Creator God is not merely an idea.

Love's instinct is to create—a work of art, literature, music or a baby. God, who created the world, loved the world so much, as John's Gospel tells us later (3:16) that he sent his only Son to offer us life. Today we celebrate the birth of Jesus. Some of us will do so with abundant food, drink and company, overflowing with joy. Some of us will struggle with memories, lost hope or loneliness. Life might feel full or empty. Regardless of our circumstances, God continues to love us and Jesus will bring us life as we open ourselves to all that he offers. It is never easy, but taking hold of God's gift of life, alongside any other presents we unwrap today, might remind us that we have been created by Love to live the best way we can with our Creator.

'Jesus is Lord, creation's voice proclaims it.' 'O come, let us adore him, Christ the Lord.' Gracious God, you created me in love. Give me the courage to choose life, and to share your life with others this Christmas.

LAKSHMI JEFFREYS

Christmas light

And the life was the light of all people. The light shines in the darkness, and the darkness did not overcome it.

You know how it is. An unexpected call of nature in the middle of the night can be irritating at the best of times. When you are in unfamiliar surroundings, unaware of the location of the light switch—or worse, when camping in the wild when there is no moonlight to guide you—how do you find your way without bumping into objects and people and waking everyone? Even the tiniest sliver of light in these cases provides assurance and hope. The darkest night is invaded by the smallest flicker of light.

Light was God's first gift in creation. God's light was rejected by the people he created and the darkness of sin and evil was introduced into the world at an early stage. This state continues. Today the church remembers Stephen, the first Christian martyr, stoned to death for speaking about Jesus as God's chosen Messiah (Acts 7). As we turn on the news, we hear of death, evil and sadness. As we remember the past year, we might recall personal unhappiness or tragedy. At this time of year such stories seem worse than ever. Darkness can feel overwhelming—yet darkness does not overcome light. Into the world as it is—full of sadness, evil, fear and despair—God sent Jesus. The life offered by the Word was its light, the light given by God to walk in. And as we know, darkness did not and does not conquer the light.

The life of Jesus, the Word, offers light to every person, regardless of circumstances. Whatever the weather is like today, perhaps you might go outside, appropriately wrapped up if necessary. (Boxing Day walks are traditional.) If this is not possible, perhaps look out of a window: there will be light somewhere. Hold yourself and your life before God, however wonderful, tired, scared or distressed you feel. How might 'the life' be 'the light' of [insert your own name]?

'The Lord is my light and my salvation; whom shall I fear?' (Psalm 27:1)
Pray through the whole of Psalm 27 and discover how God's light will shine into the darkness.

LAKSHMI JEFFREYS

Mission possible?

There was a man sent from God, whose name was John. He came as a witness to testify to the light, so that all might believe through him.

At the age of 10, our son was introduced to the Mission Impossible series of films. Full of gadgets and action, they are perfect viewing for children of any age from 10 to over 100! The hero is given a seemingly impossible task (the instructions then 'self-destruct'); a group of unlikely colleagues gathers and completes the task with seconds to spare, thwarting the villain who wanted to take over the world. The films will almost certainly be shown somewhere on television this Christmas.

The task of John the Baptist was different. Sent by God, John prepared people for Jesus, baptised Jesus and died in such circumstances that King Herod, hearing about Jesus, thought that John the Baptist had come back to life. John was not a Hollywood hero with state-of-the art equipment and a troop of 'rough diamonds'. He had to play his part and then step aside as the real hero took centre stage. He was a witness, confirming what Jesus would say about himself, reminding people of all that the Old Testament prophets had said concerning God's promised Messiah.

The mission of all Christians is the same as that of the Baptist: to be a witness to testify to the light. Although we are called by God, you and I are not to be the star: we are simply those who point to Jesus, the true hero. This does not sound demanding but, for many of us, it can be challenging in practice. We can shirk our responsibility to those who need our testimony to encounter the light for themselves. We seek elaborate techniques and training rather than sharing our lives and stories. We are tempted to give up when the mission is difficult. The mission is possible only when we remember who called us and equips us and will be with us as we proceed. John the Baptist knew God, so he understood his task. Do we?

The post-Christmas sales involve shoppers on a mission to obtain the best bargains. The mission of a Christian is less seasonal but requires equal endurance and focus.

LAKSHMI JEFFREYS

True enlightenment

He himself was not the light, but he came to testify to the light. The true light, which enlightens everyone, was coming into the world.

The word 'world' in John's Gospel often has negative connotations: the world is under judgement (3:19), requires salvation (4:42) and hates Jesus (7:7). The world is a place in which people prefer darkness to light. There has never been a time in history when people did not seek power over others, destroy much of the world's beauty in a quest to dominate, cause grief and anger through thoughtless and careless words and actions, or demand retribution rather than offering mercy and forgiveness. Today many churches will recall King Herod's massacre of babies when he learned of Jesus' birth ('the slaughter of the innocents'). Meanwhile, this week's news broadcasts will have revealed ineffectual or despotic world leaders, financial mismanagement, murder, cruelty and celebrity worship. As in the time of John, society today needs enlightenment.

John himself was not the light—and was probably profoundly grateful of it. After all, who wants the job of sorting out our world? He pointed to the true light. The inclusion of the word 'true' is important because not all light is helpful. Lamp-posts near airports are shorter than those on other streets so that, in foggy or snowy conditions, pilots do not mistake them for runway lights. 'Even Satan disguises himself as an angel of light' (2 Corinthians 11:14). John's role was to remind or show people who Jesus was. Jesus, the Word of God, was and is the light of the world, the way, who enlightens everyone, whether or not we take any notice.

Between Christmas and New Year there are many reflections on the year that has passed—who has died or achieved significance or notoriety; important events; amusing asides; bizarre occasions. There is also much talk about the coming year, with predictions of what might happen to individuals, nations or even the world as a whole. Perhaps one role of Christians is to pray for situations and people in the news who particularly need to be enlightened. At the same time, we can ask Jesus to shed true light on our lives, that we may see clearly and proceed wisely.

Loving Jesus, enlighten everyone with true light.

LAKSHMI JEFFREYS

Reality check

He was in the world, and the world came into being through him; yet the world did not know him. He came to what was his own, and his own people did not accept him.

Once again John puts together the cosmic and the personal: he (an individual) was one man in the world that he (God) had created. The 'world' (with negative connotations again), directed to evil by human sin, rejected him. He came to his own land, to the people chosen by God, those who for centuries had been prepared for his coming by Moses and the prophets—but those people refused to accept him.

In general, people want life on their terms. Too much 'reality' is beyond the endurance of most of us, so we ignore or deny it. One of the most difficult situations I encounter in my job is when an individual has been bereaved but refuses to accept at some level that their loved one has died. Grieving parents will place birthday cards on graves, showing the age their child would be, had he or she lived. They cannot bear to acknowledge that their 'baby', however old, has died, so the birthday cards celebrate the age reached in life. A widow does not want her husband of decades to have died. She lives with her reality until someone or something reminds her that he is no longer around, at which point she plummets into depression or flies into a rage. In either case, anyone or anything that shatters the illusion is considered cruel and unfeeling.

Perhaps this is why Jesus was not accepted on earth. He, more than anyone else, would offer reality: He is the way, the truth and the life. An encounter with Jesus showed the individual who they really were. The rich young ruler discovered that his attachment to wealth was stronger than his desire for eternal life. On the other hand, Zacchaeus discovered that Jesus accepted him and, as a result, he was transformed. The Creator God comes to you and to me. Will we accept him on his terms?

People sometimes say that God does not care. Perhaps it is not God who is indifferent; perhaps people refuse to recognise the way life is, living in their own fantasy world until reality hits.

LAKSHMI JEFFREYS

The power of becoming God's child

But to all who received him, who believed in his name, he gave power to become children of God, who were born, not of blood or of the will of the flesh or of the will of man, but of God.

By the time she was seven years old, Annie (not her real name) had lived in various homes with half a dozen different families, including at least one couple who adopted, then betrayed her. Her teenage years were especially turbulent as she wrestled with issues of identity—so much harder to manage when she had not known love and stability in her early life. In no small way through the ceaseless care of her permanent adoptive parents and the prayers and practical support of her church community, she eventually experienced a miraculous total conversion to faith in and discipleship of Jesus Christ. The young woman who at one point had been on a self-destructive downward spiral wrote the following words: 'I want to live a blessed life, blessing others in return. I want to have a pure heart and live pleasingly to God and others. I want them to see the light of Jesus shine from me without having to whisper a word.' Annie expressed exquisitely what happens when a person receives Jesus and experiences the power to become a child of God.

In the Gospel of John, to believe is to accept Jesus and what he claims to be, and then to dedicate your life to him. Belief in Jesus offers status—becoming a child of God. As one person said, 'Nobodies become somebodies, regardless of how they see themselves.' This is in complete contrast to yesterday's reading about those who could not cope with the real world. Annie discovered that believing in Jesus because God believed in her gave her dignity and a reason to live fully. God is not beyond any circumstances in which we find ourselves.

Loving God, human birth has human initiatives—the will of the flesh or the will of man. Becoming a child of yours means that you have taken the initiative in love. Thank you for coming to us, accepting us as we are and offering us the best way to live.

LAKSHMI JEFFREYS

On the brink of a new beginning

And the Word became flesh and lived among us, and we have seen his glory, the glory as of a father's only son, full of grace and truth.

Among other things, 2018 marks the 100th anniversary of the end of World War I. A documentary was made entitled *World War I—the Death of Glory*. This conflict, called 'the Great War' and supposed to end all wars, was characterised by weaponry and attitudes that displaced chivalry and honour, leading to the deaths of millions of people and another global conflict less than a quarter of a century later. History suggests that glory was far from present. A century later, it is interesting to look back and discover what, if anything, we have seen or learned about glory.

In our reading, God's glory is linked to grace and truth. In turn, they echo God's assent to Moses' request to see that glory, in Exodus 33:19: 'I will cause all my goodness to pass in front of you... I will have mercy on whom I will have mercy, and I will have compassion on whom I will have compassion' (NIV). Grace is an undeserved and often unlooked-for expression of God's compassion and mercy. There is something in today's verse from John 1 about Jesus as the physical embodiment of the glory of God experienced by Moses—Jesus who described himself as 'the truth' as well as the way and the life.

Tomorrow is the beginning of a new year. At the beginning of this series of readings, we saw the cosmic and the personal together. As 2018 is about to begin, you might consider reading through the whole of John's prologue and perhaps look back over 2017 to see how Jesus has been with you since the beginning. Use this knowledge to hold before God the coming year and your hopes, dreams and fears. My prayer is that you and I will experience God's compassion and mercy as we look into the face of Jesus Christ. The infant whose birth we celebrate in this season will remain with us in the days, weeks and months to come.

Gracious Creator God, as 2018 begins, show me your glory in Jesus,
that I may walk with him in grace and truth during the year.

LAKSHMI JEFFREYS

Reading *New Daylight* in a group

SALLY WELCH

I am aware that although some of you cherish the moments of quiet during the day that enable you to read and reflect on the passages we offer you in *New Daylight*, other readers prefer to study in small groups, to enable conversation and discussion and the sharing of insights. With this in mind, here are some ideas for discussion starters within a study group. Some of the questions are generic and can be applied to any set of contributions within this issue; others are specific to certain sets of readings. I hope they generate some interesting reflections and conversations.

General discussion starters

These questions can be used for any study series within this issue. Remember, there are no right or wrong answers; they are intended simply to enable a group to engage in conversation.

- What do you think is the main idea or theme of the author in this series? Do you think the writer succeeded in communicating this idea to you, or were you more interested in the side issues?

- Have you had any experience of the issues that are raised in the study? How have they affected your life?

- What evidence does the author use to support their ideas? Do they use personal observations and experience, facts, or quotations from other authorities? Which appeals to you most?

- Does the author make a 'call to action'? Is that call realistic and achievable? Do you think their ideas will work in the secular world?

- Can you identify specific passages that struck you personally—as interesting, profound, difficult to understand or illuminating?

- Did you learn something new from reading this series? Will you think differently about some things, and if so, what are they?

Mental health (Harry Smart)

Harry writes very powerfully about the different approaches to mental health that can be found in the Bible. How useful has this been to you? Which of the attitudes have you noticed in today's world? How can Jesus' attitude towards those in mental distress help us today? How challenged are you by mental health issues in yourself or in others?

Angels (Margaret Silf)

Do the angels in the Bible seem real to you? How different are their approaches? What is your reaction to the mention of angels in everyday life? Have you had any experience of angels? What form have they taken? How were they received? How might you serve as an angel in your community—is this the same thing?

Reflective question (Wilderness, Nick Read)

In the introduction to his notes, Nick writes that 'wilderness is where the challenges presented by the environment bring issues of faith into focus'. How have your 'wilderness moments' shaped or challenged your faith?

Author profile: David Winter

David Winter is known and loved by many as author and broadcaster, and is a particular favourite with *New Daylight* readers. Here we discover more about his life and ministry.

David, what led you to become ordained?

I was ordained deacon in 1987 (with the first women to be ordained in London diocese) and priested in 1988. The longest part of my working life was in journalism and broadcasting, including 20 years as a producer at the BBC, and finally Head of Religious Broadcasting. I took slightly early retirement from the BBC and came to the Oxford diocese as Diocesan Missioner and parish priest of Ducklington, near Witney. Heaven on earth! So I've clocked up 28 years as a priest (which still surprises me).

You've been a priest now for many years and served in lots of different ways. Can you tell us about some of the highlights?

Every bit of ministry has been rewarding, but I think ministering to people who are facing death (the thought of which I had dreaded) has probably been the most rewarding of all. I suppose it's also the most 'challenging' (by which we usually mean 'difficult'). At the moment I find taking services in inadequately lit churches very 'challenging'!

How did you get involved with writing for *New Daylight* and how do you find the experience of writing Bible study notes?

Shelagh Brown, who was then editing *New Daylight*, approached me when I left the BBC, so I think I've been doing it for about 27 years, including a couple of hectic years when I took over as emergency editor after Shelagh's untimely death. I love writing the notes: I find the whole experience a personal blessing. I've discovered that however well you think you know a passage of scripture, there's always more to come from it.

Do you have an unfulfilled wish or ambition?

At my advanced years I don't have any ambitions except to make a good death!

One final question: what would you like your tombstone to say?

I know what will be on my tombstone, because I shall be buried with my beloved wife, who died in 2001. It simply says, 'With Christ'. What more could one ask?

Recommended reading

BRF's 2017 Advent book leads us through December and up to Epiphany with the famous songs of Jesus' birth in Luke's Gospel, plus further songs from the New Testament. The author is the acclaimed writer and speaker **Derek Tidball**. The following extract is from the Introduction and the reading for 2 December.

In our house, Christmas is always a time for music. We rejoice in going to concerts, buying new recordings of old carols with their familiar words and tunes and equally welcome new compositions, or new collections of our favourite performers. Christmas without music is as inconceivable as Christmas without presents or turkey...

Soaked in the older scriptures of the Jewish people, the songs Luke records in his inspired Gospel—the songs of Mary, Zechariah, Simeon, and the angels at Bethlehem—reveal the wondrous depths that for us 'in the town of David, a Saviour has been born to us. He is the Messiah' (Luke 2:11). Their words are often those of the Old Testament, their style one of passionate yet reverent worship; their tone is one of humility, yet their rhythm indicates confident upbeat praise...

Let me ask a personal question. Do you like looking through keyholes? It is probably not the done thing to admit to such curiosity in polite company but the truth is many of us are pretty inquisitive... This book invites us to treat the songs of the Saviour's birth as keyholes through which we can spy amazing things. As we peep through our metaphorical keyholes, our eyes don't immediately settle on a crib or a crying infant. They lead us first to view the whole story of God's dealings with Israel that has led to the arrival of the Saviour. They lead us through pain, agony and failure, to discover the faithful mercy of God who, in sending a baby to Bethlehem, gives hope to his people and the wider world. We get to the manger, but only after negotiating our way through a longer story first...

Each day's comment is concluded with a text on which the reader is encouraged to meditate. To meditate is to fill our minds with truth from God or about God and to chew it over in our thinking. Five questions may help us to get started. What does this text mean? What does it teach about God? How far do I believe what it states? What difficulties do I have with this text and how can I overcome them? How does it apply to me today?

2 December: Daughter of grace

Read Luke 1:26–45.

Not infrequently, the songs that rise to the top of the charts today are not original creations, but fresh recordings by new artists of songs that have been around for a good time. A new voice, new arrangements, instruments, and technology, give the songs from long ago a new lease of life. Sometimes triggered by the personal experience of the new artist, they are creative re-presentations to communicate to a changing situation. So it was, in part, with Mary's song.

Mary is one of a long line of women in Israel for whom giving birth is the crucial issue. From Sarah, through Rachel and Hannah, down to cousin Elizabeth, we learn of several childless women who miraculously conceive and whose children not only bring joy to the family but go on to play a critical role in securing the future of Israel. Unlike these women, Mary is not infertile. She's a young, vulnerable teenager who is a virgin (Luke 1:27, 34). Since she has not yet married, her virginity is a virtue, not a matter of shame. No wonder that when the news that she will conceive a child is brought to her by the angel Gabriel, she's confused and 'troubled'. With apparently no one to turn to, she goes to visit her older cousin Elizabeth, who is also surprisingly pregnant, knowing that they'd at least have something in common. While she is there, she bursts into song—the song we know as the Magnificat, because it glorifies the Lord.

Was Mary's song original? Not exactly. It shows great similarities to Hannah's song after she had given birth to Samuel (1 Samuel 2:1–10). Their songs celebrate God's gracious initiative in coming to the rescue of Israel through the birth of a child. Hannah's 'prayer represents a turning point in Israel's history. It closed an age which at times bordered on anarchy, a period of shame and humiliation… [and] opened the door to Israel's greatness.' What happened under Samuel was merely a pointer to the greater achievements that would occur with the coming of Jesus.

Mary does not draw on Hannah's song alone. Line after line cascading from her lips comes from the Psalms, including Psalms 34, 35, 89 and 103. She may be young and female, and therefore probably uneducated, but she is devout. These psalms would have been sung sabbath after sabbath in the Nazareth synagogue and she has imbibed them deeply in her spirit. They have become a part of her. So, when the occasion arises, the appropriate words are all to hand, woven into a fresh new tapestry.

After the opening declaration ('My soul magnifies the Lord'), God is the subject of every sentence. The song does not boast that she is to become a mother, but rather that God, the Mighty One, is coming to the rescue, being merciful to Israel and proving faithful to his promise. We would have understood if the song expressed some angst about her sudden and unexpected condition. What will happen to her? What will people's reactions be? How will she cope? Yet the song is remarkably free from her own concerns and worries and astonishingly focused on God. God must be the starting point for all our faith. If we have a wrong view of him, we will have a distorted and probably dysfunctional faith.

When she does briefly speak of herself, she is not the subject, not centre stage. God still remains the subject. He is the giver and she is the surprising recipient of his grace. Her 'lowliness' isn't pseudo-humility but actual fact. From what we know of her, as a young teenage girl, she wasn't significant in other people's eyes. She also seems to have been relatively poor, judging by the offering that she and Joseph made in the temple (Luke 2:24). Coming from that backwater, Nazareth, she really was insignificant. She didn't merit any particular attention. Without qualification or entitlement, God chose her to be the mother of his incarnate son. She was 'blessed' indeed, as God poured his grace into her life.

What a remarkable thing for God to do, to trust the salvation of the world to a vulnerable, unwed teenage girl and, eventually, to Joseph, who was probably nothing much to be proud of either as a manual labourer from Nazareth. But that's the extraordinary thing about God. It is the way he has always worked. He didn't choose the nation of Israel for its strength or size (Deuteronomy 7:7–9) and he doesn't choose us because we're somebodies, but rather because we're nobodies (1 Corinthians 1:26–29). Mary fits the picture. She is honoured because she is the daughter of God's amazing grace.

Like Mary, we have no cause to boast in ourselves but only in the grace of God. I wonder if, like her, we're so steeped in scripture that we have the vocabulary to express the wonder of that grace.

For meditation:

'Blessed are the poor in spirit, for theirs is the kingdom of heaven' (Matthew 5:3).

To order a copy of this book, please turn to the order form on page 149.

Books from familiar authors

We have a number of books recently published or about to be published, written by authors who may be familiar to you. Whether you have a passion for prayer or pilgrimage, there's something for everyone with our wide variety of topics. Develop your understanding or learn something entirely new!

The Recovery of Joy

Finding the path from rootlessness to returning home

NAOMI STARKEY
pb, 978 0 85746 518 4 £7.99

Naomi Starkey, the previous editor of *New Daylight*, is back with another amazing title. Using a refreshing and unusual blend of story and biblical exposition, she traces a journey that begins in rootlessness and despair and takes a wanderer across the sea to a series of islands. These islands are the setting for a series of events and encounters through which the wanderer emerges from that initial rootlessness and makes a progression through healing to a rediscovery of the joy of feeling at the centre of God's loving purpose. *The Recovery of Joy* shows how we can find a path back to connection with God, the source of joy, even from the bleakest points of life.

Experiencing Christ's Love

Establishing a life of worship, prayer, study, service and reflection

JOHN TWISLETON
pb, 978 0 85746 517 7 £7.99

In this new title, John Twisleton, a familiar BRF author, reminds us of Jesus' gracious challenge to love God with heart, soul and mind, and to love our neighbour as ourselves. Against the backdrop of the message of God's unconditional love in

Jesus Christ, he delivers a wake-up call to the basic Christian patterns of worship, prayer, study, service and reflection. These, he claims, serve to take God's hand in ours, leading us into his divine possibilities.

Pilgrim Journeys

Pilgrimage for walkers and armchair travellers

SALLY WELCH
pb, 978 0 85746 513 9 £8.99

The current editor of *New Daylight*, Sally Welch, has written this guide to pilgrimage, for those who wish to make a physical journey and for so-called 'armchair travellers'. The book explores the less travelled pilgrim routes of the UK and beyond.

Each chapter explores a different aspect of pilgrimage, offering reflections and indicating some of the spiritual lessons to be learned from pilgrimage, that may be practised at home. This absorbing book shows how insights gained on the journey can be incorporated into everyday life, bringing new ways of relationship with God and with our fellow Christians, offering support and encouragement as we face life's joys and challenges.

Facing Death

RACHEL BOULDING
978 0 85746 564 1 £3.99

Rachel Boulding's notes from the May 2016 issue of *New Daylight* have been expanded and made available in our 'Bible readings for special times' series, by popular demand. Many readers found Rachel's honest and insightful thoughts about facing her own diagnosis touching and inspiring. With moving vulnerability and without denying the difficult reality of the situation, Rachel suggests a way to confront terminal illness with faith and hope in a loving God.

500th anniversary of the Lutheran Reformation

Praying the Bible with Luther
A simple approach to everyday prayer

MICHAEL PARSONS
978 0 85746 503 0   £8.99

Michael Parsons, one of BRF's commissioning editors, has written this book exploring how to pray through the Bible in the same way that Luther did. With the 500th anniversary of the Lutheran Reformation taking place this year, this book is ideally placed not only to give information about who Luther was but also to suggest a new way of praying and engaging with the Bible.

Beginning each time of prayer with a Bible passage, Luther would meditate on it with four 'strands' in mind: teaching, thanksgiving, repentance and supplication. Then he would pray, having his thoughts shaped by his reading, praying God's words after him, confident of God's grace. *Praying the Bible with Luther* explains this method, demonstrates it and encourages readers to follow Luther's example, helping us to turn scripture into prayer and to pray it into our own lives today.

This is more than a simple approach to everyday prayer, it's a deep book for those who desire to be serious about prayer. Highly commended for use personally and with small groups.

DAVID COFFEY OBE, GLOBAL AMBASSADOR, BMS WORLD MISSION

To order a copy of any of the books featured above, please use the order form on page 149. BRF books are also available from your local Christian bookshop or from **brfonline.org.uk**

To order

Online: brfonline.org.uk
Telephone: +44 (0)1865 319700
Mon–Fri 9.15–17.30

Delivery times within the UK are normally
15 working days. Prices are correct at the time of
going to press but may change without prior notice.

Title	Price	Qty	Total
Christmas through the Keyhole	£6.99		
The Recovery of Joy	£7.99		
Experiencing Christ's Love	£7.99		
Pilgrim Journeys	£8.99		
Facing Death	£3.99		
Praying the Bible with Luther	£8.99		

POSTAGE AND PACKING CHARGES			
Order value	UK	Europe	Rest of world
Under £7.00	£1.25	£3.00	£5.50
£7.00–£29.99	£2.25	£5.50	£10.00
£30.00 and over	FREE	Prices on request	

Total value of books	
Postage and packing	
Total for this order	

Please complete in BLOCK CAPITALS

Title .... First name/initials .... Surname ....

Address ....

.... Postcode ....

Acc. No. .... Telephone ....

Email ....

Please keep me informed about BRF's books and resources ❑ by email ❑ by post
Please keep me informed about the wider work of BRF ❑ by email ❑ by post

Method of payment

❑ Cheque (made payable to BRF) ❑ MasterCard / Visa

Card no. ❑❑❑❑ ❑❑❑❑ ❑❑❑❑ ❑❑❑❑ ❑❑❑❑ ❑❑

Valid from ❑❑ ❑❑ Expires ❑❑ ❑❑ Security code* ❑❑❑

Last 3 digits on the reverse of the card

Signature* .... Date ..../............/............

*ESSENTIAL IN ORDER TO PROCESS YOUR ORDER

Please return this form to: BRF, 15 The Chambers, Vineyard, Abingdon OX14 3FE | enquiries@brf.org.uk
To read our terms and find out about cancelling your order, please visit **brfonline.org.uk/terms**.

The Bible Reading Fellowship (BRF) is a Registered Charity (233280)

How to encourage Bible reading in your church

BRF has been helping individuals connect with the Bible for over 90 years. We want to support churches as they seek to encourage church members into regular Bible reading.

Order a Bible reading resources pack

This pack is designed to give your church the tools to publicise our Bible reading notes. It includes:

- Sample Bible reading notes for your congregation to try.
- Publicity resources, including a poster.
- A church magazine feature about Bible reading notes.

The pack is free, but we welcome a £5 donation to cover the cost of postage. If you require a pack to be sent outside the UK or require a specific number of sample Bible reading notes, please contact us for postage costs. More information about what the current pack contains is available on our website.

How to order and find out more

- Visit **biblereadingnotes.org.uk/for-churches**
- Telephone BRF on +44 (0)1865 319700 Mon–Fri 9.15–17.30
- Write to us at BRF, 15 The Chambers, Vineyard, Abingdon OX14 3FE

Keep informed about our latest initiatives

We are continuing to develop resources to help churches encourage people into regular Bible reading, wherever they are on their journey. Join our email list at **biblereadingnotes.org.uk/helpingchurches** to stay informed about the latest initiatives that your church could benefit from.

Introduce a friend to our notes

We can send information about our notes and current prices for you to pass on. Please contact us.

BRF Transforming Lives and Communities

BRF is a charity that is passionate about making a difference through the Christian faith. We want to see lives and communities transformed through our creative programmes and resources for individuals, churches and schools. We are doing this by resourcing:

- **Christian growth and understanding of the Bible.** Through our Bible reading notes, books, digital resources, Quiet Days and other events, we're resourcing individuals, groups and leaders in churches for their own spiritual journey and for their ministry.

- **Church outreach in the local community.** BRF is the home of three programmes that churches are embracing to great effect as they seek to engage with their local communities: Messy Church, Who Let The Dads Out? and The Gift of Years.

- **Teaching Christianity in primary schools.** Our Barnabas in Schools team is working with primary-aged children and their teachers, enabling them to explore Christianity creatively within the school curriculum.

- **Children's and family ministry.** Through our Barnabas in Churches and Faith in Homes websites and published resources, we're working with churches and families, enabling children under 11, and the adults working with them, to explore Christianity creatively and bring the Bible alive.

Do you share our vision?

Sales of our books and Bible reading notes cover the cost of producing them. However, our other programmes are funded primarily by donations, grants and legacies. If you share our vision, would you help us to transform even more lives and communities? Your prayers and financial support are vital for the work that we do.

- You could support BRF's ministry with a one-off gift or regular donation (using the response form on page 153).

- You could consider making a bequest to BRF in your will (page 152).

- You could encourage your church to support BRF as part of your church's giving to home mission—perhaps focusing on a specific area of our ministry, or a particular member of our Barnabas team.

- Most important of all, you could support BRF with your prayers.

Make a lasting difference through a gift in your will

 What do we want our children to care about as they grow and take their place in society? It's a big issue and one that The Bible Reading Fellowship (BRF) cares about deeply.

One of the ways in which we seek to address this issue is by teaching Christianity in primary schools. Our Barnabas in Schools team works with primary-aged children and their teachers, enabling them to explore Christianity creatively and confidently within the school curriculum. 33,000 children experience our Barnabas RE Days each year.

The schools team recently introduced two special Barnabas RE Days called 'Creating Character'. These explore the Christian values of Friendship, Forgiveness and Peace; and Compassion, Service and Community. In an age of uncertainty, we want to help shape a generation of people who are more tolerant and loving of each other.

Since BRF's story began in 1922, we have been making a difference through the Christian faith. Today our creative programmes and resources for schools, individuals and churches impact the lives of thousands of individuals across the UK and overseas. This is thanks, in large part, to the generosity of those who have supported us during their lifetime and through gifts in wills.

If you share our passion for making a difference through the Christian faith, please consider leaving a gift in your will to BRF. Gifts in wills are an important source of income for us and they don't need to be huge to make a real difference. For every £1 we receive, we invest 95p back into charitable activities. Just imagine what we could do over the next century with your help.

For further information about making a gift to BRF in your will, please visit **brf.org.uk/lastingdifference** or contact Sophie on 01865 319700 or email giving@brf.org.uk.

Whatever you can do or give, we thank you for your support.

SHARING OUR VISION – MAKING A GIFT

I would like to make a gift to support BRF. Please use my gift for:

☐ where it is needed most ☐ Barnabas Children's Ministry

☐ Messy Church ☐ Who Let The Dads Out? ☐ The Gift of Years

Title	First name/initials	Surname	
Address			
			Postcode
Email			
Telephone			
Signature			Date

giftaid it You can add an extra 25p to every £1 you give.

Please treat as Gift Aid donations all qualifying gifts of money made

☐ today, ☐ in the past four years, ☐ and in the future.

I am a UK taxpayer and understand that if I pay less Income Tax and/or Capital Gains Tax in the current tax year than the amount of Gift Aid claimed on all my donations, it is my responsibility to pay any difference.

☐ My donation does not qualify for Gift Aid.

Please notify BRF if you want to cancel this Gift Aid declaration, change your name or home address, or no longer pay sufficient tax on your income and/or capital gains.

Please complete other side of form ➡

Please return this form to:
BRF, 15 The Chambers, Vineyard, Abingdon OX14 3FE

The Bible Reading Fellowship is a Registered Charity (233280)

SHARING OUR VISION – MAKING A GIFT

Regular giving

By Direct Debit:

☐ I would like to make a regular gift of £ [   ] per month/quarter/year.
Please also complete the Direct Debit instruction on page 159.

By Standing Order:

Please contact Priscilla Kew +44 (0)1235 462305 | giving@brf.org.uk

One-off donation

Please accept my gift of:

☐ £10 ☐ £50 ☐ £100 Other £ [   ]

by (delete as appropriate):

☐ Cheque/Charity Voucher payable to 'BRF'

☐ MasterCard/Visa/Debit card/Charity card

Name on card

Card no. [ ][ ][ ][ ] [ ][ ][ ][ ] [ ][ ][ ][ ] [ ][ ][ ][ ]

Valid from [M][M] [Y][Y] Expires [M][M] [Y][Y]

Security code* [ ][ ][ ] *Last 3 digits on the reverse of the card
ESSENTIAL IN ORDER TO PROCESS YOUR PAYMENT

Signature   Date

We like to acknowledge all donations. However, if you do not wish to receive
an acknowledgement, please tick here ☐

↻ Please complete other side of form

Please return this form to:
BRF, 15 The Chambers, Vineyard, Abingdon OX14 3FE

BRF

The Bible Reading Fellowship is a Registered Charity (233280)

ND0317

NEW DAYLIGHT SUBSCRIPTION RATES

Please note our subscription rates, current until April 2018:

Individual subscriptions
covering 3 issues for under 5 copies, payable in advance
(including postage & packing):

	UK	Europe	Rest of world
New Daylight	£16.50	£24.60	£28.50
New Daylight 3-year subscription (9 issues) (not available for Deluxe)	£45.00	N/A	N/A
New Daylight Deluxe per set of 3 issues p.a.	£20.85	£33.45	£40.50

Group subscriptions
covering 3 issues for 5 copies or more, sent to **one** UK address (post free):

New Daylight	£13.20 per set of 3 issues p.a.
New Daylight Deluxe	£16.95 per set of 3 issues p.a.

Please note that the annual billing period for group subscriptions runs from 1 May to 30 April.

Overseas group subscription rates
Available on request. Please email enquiries@brf.org.uk.

Copies may also be obtained from Christian bookshops:

New Daylight	£4.40 per copy
New Daylight Deluxe	£5.65 per copy

All our Bible reading notes can be ordered online by visiting
biblereadingnotes.org.uk/subscriptions

For information about our other Bible reading notes,
and apps for iPhone and iPod touch, visit
biblereadingnotes.org.uk

NEW DAYLIGHT INDIVIDUAL SUBSCRIPTION FORM

All our Bible reading notes can be ordered online by visiting
biblereadingnotes.org.uk/subscriptions

☐ I would like to take out a subscription:

Title .... First name/initials .... Surname ....

Address ....

.... Postcode ....

Telephone .... Email ....

Please send *New Daylight* beginning with the January 2018 / May 2018 / September 2018 issue (*delete as appropriate*):

(*please tick box*)	UK	Europe	Rest of world
New Daylight	☐ £16.50	☐ £24.60	☐ £28.50
New Daylight 3-year subscription	☐ £45.00	N/A	N/A
New Daylight Deluxe	☐ £20.85	☐ £33.45	☐ £40.50

Total enclosed £ .... (cheques should be made payable to 'BRF')

Please charge my MasterCard / Visa ☐ Debit card ☐ with £ ....

Card no. ☐☐☐☐ ☐☐☐☐ ☐☐☐☐ ☐☐☐☐

Valid from ☐☐ ☐☐   Expires ☐☐ ☐☐   Security code* ☐☐☐

Last 3 digits on the reverse of the card

Signature* .... Date ...... / ...... / ......

*ESSENTIAL IN ORDER TO PROCESS YOUR PAYMENT

To set up a Direct Debit, please also complete the Direct Debit instruction on page 159 and return it to BRF with this form.

Please return this form with the appropriate payment to:
BRF, 15 The Chambers, Vineyard, Abingdon OX14 3FE

To read our terms and find out about cancelling your order, please visit **brfonline.org.uk/terms**.

The Bible Reading Fellowship is a Registered Charity (233280)

ND0317

NEW DAYLIGHT GIFT SUBSCRIPTION FORM

☐ I would like to give a gift subscription (please provide both names and addresses):

Title .... First name/initials .... Surname ....

Address ....

.... Postcode ....

Telephone .... Email ....

Gift subscription name ....

Gift subscription address ....

.... Postcode ....

Gift message (20 words max. or include your own gift card):

....

....

Please send *New Daylight* beginning with the January 2018 / May 2018 / September 2018 issue (*delete as appropriate*):

(please tick box)	UK	Europe	Rest of world
New Daylight	☐ £16.50	☐ £24.60	☐ £28.50
New Daylight 3-year subscription	☐ £45.00	N/A	N/A
New Daylight Deluxe	☐ £20.85	☐ £33.45	☐ £40.50

Total enclosed £ .... (cheques should be made payable to 'BRF')

Please charge my MasterCard / Visa ☐ Debit card ☐ with £ ....

Card no. ☐☐☐☐ ☐☐☐☐ ☐☐☐☐ ☐☐☐☐

Valid from ☐☐ ☐☐ Expires ☐☐ ☐☐ Security code* ☐☐☐

Last 3 digits on the reverse of the card

Signature* .... Date ...... / ...... / ......

*ESSENTIAL IN ORDER TO PROCESS YOUR PAYMENT

To set up a Direct Debit, please also complete the Direct Debit instruction on page 159 and return it to BRF with this form.

Please return this form with the appropriate payment to:
BRF, 15 The Chambers, Vineyard, Abingdon OX14 3FE

To read our terms and find out about cancelling your order, please visit **brfonline.org.uk/terms**.

The Bible Reading Fellowship is a Registered Charity (233280)

DIRECT DEBIT PAYMENT

You can pay for your annual subscription to our Bible reading notes using Direct Debit. You need only give your bank details once, and the payment is made automatically every year until you cancel it. If you would like to pay by Direct Debit, please use the form opposite, entering your BRF account number under 'Reference number'.

You are fully covered by the Direct Debit Guarantee:

The Direct Debit Guarantee

- This Guarantee is offered by all banks and building societies that accept instructions to pay Direct Debits.

- If there are any changes to the amount, date or frequency of your Direct Debit, The Bible Reading Fellowship will notify you 10 working days in advance of your account being debited or as otherwise agreed. If you request The Bible Reading Fellowship to collect a payment, confirmation of the amount and date will be given to you at the time of the request.

- If an error is made in the payment of your Direct Debit, by The Bible Reading Fellowship or your bank or building society, you are entitled to a full and immediate refund of the amount paid from your bank or building society.

- If you receive a refund you are not entitled to, you must pay it back when The Bible Reading Fellowship asks you to.

- You can cancel a Direct Debit at any time by simply contacting your bank or building society. Written confirmation may be required. Please also notify us.

The Bible Reading Fellowship

Instruction to your bank or building society to pay by Direct Debit

Please fill in the whole form using a ballpoint pen and return it to:
BRF, 15 The Chambers, Vineyard, Abingdon OX14 3FE

Service User Number:

5	5	8	2	2	9

Name and full postal address of your bank or building society

To: The Manager	Bank/Building Society
Address	
	Postcode

Name(s) of account holder(s)

Branch sort code

Bank/Building Society account number

Reference number

Instruction to your Bank/Building Society

Please pay The Bible Reading Fellowship Direct Debits from the account detailed
in this instruction, subject to the safeguards assured by the Direct Debit Guarantee.
I understand that this instruction may remain with The Bible Reading Fellowship
and, if so, details will be passed electronically to my bank/building society.

Signature(s)

Banks and Building Societies may not accept Direct Debit instructions for some types
of account.

This page is left blank for your notes.